St. John

Off The Beaten Track

A Unique and Unusual Guide to St. John, U.S.V.I.

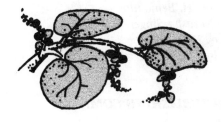

By Gerald Singer

SECOND EDITION, REVISED

Printed in the United States of America
Library of Congress Catalog Card Number 96-92640
ISBN # 0-9641220-1-4

Written by Gerald Singer
Edited by Constance Wallace

Foreword by Guy H. Benjamin
Illustrated by Natasha Singer
Photographs by Dean Hulse
Cover design by Michael Barry

SOMBRERO PUBLISHING COMPANY
P.O. Box 1031
St. John, United States Virgin Islands, 00831-1031

e mail: gsinger@islands.vi

Contents

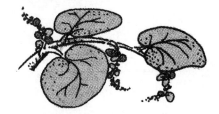

Contents

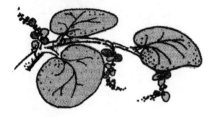

Contents

SECTION FOUR: BEACHES AND SNORKELING

CONTENTS

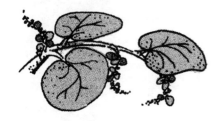

NATURAL HISTORY

FOREWORD

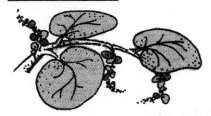

Treasures come in all sizes, shapes and colors. Mr. Gerald Singer has given us a fitting treasure in *St. John, Off The Beaten Track,* with history, folk tales, beauties of nature, the best places to relax and wonder and the scenic vistas that make St. John the pearl of places.

Whether you swim, snorkel, dream, interact with nature, love solitude, love people or just want to be you, take *St. John, Off The Beaten Track* along with you. Read it at your leisure. Meet the liar from Johnny Horn or the swimmers from Leinster Bay to "Freedom" in Tortola. Go to Rams Head or the Peace Hill. You have a treat in store. Enjoy!

Guy H. Benjamin

Guy H. Benjamin was born in East End, St. John. He was the first St. Johnian to graduate from the Charlotte Amalie High School in St. Thomas. He received his B.A. from Howard University and his master's degree from New York University. Upon returning to the Virgin Islands, he dedicated himself to a career in education. In recognition of his contribution to education in the Virgin Islands, the name of the Benjamin Franklin School was changed to the Guy H. Benjamin School by the Virgin Island legislature.

Guy Benjamin is the author of *Me and My Beloved Virgin*, published in 1981, and *More Tales From Me and My Beloved Virgin*, published in 1983.

Acknowledgments

I would like to express my heartfelt gratitude to the warm and tolerant people of St. John who, even though I came from some-where else, have made me feel like a member of their family.

And to the people who have contributed to the making of this book such as Les Anderson, Ellen Bartfeld, Mano Boyd, Curtney Chinnery, Ethien Chinnery, Ivan Chinnery, Charlie Deyalsingh, Denise George, Eleanor Gibney, John Gibney, Holly Henkel, Dean Hulse, Wilmouth King, Rachel Rothenberg, Natasha Singer, Ross Singer, Hermon Smith and to any others whom I have forgotten to mention.

Special thanks to Constance Wallace for her sharp editing skills, bright mind, sense of humor, and the energy and enthusiasm she brought to this project.

SAFETY CONSIDERATIONS

On trails

It is always safer to hike the trails with at least one other person. If you have a problem, there will be someone there to help. Along the same lines, it is recommended that you let someone know of your hiking plans, such as, where you are going and approximately when you expect to return.

The weather on St. John is generally sunny and hot. Bring water. A half a gallon per person for a four-hour hike is recommended. Don't drink the water in the guts along the trails. Avoid fatigue by maintaining a slow pace especially up hills. Protect yourself from the sun. It is a good idea to use a strong sun block, reapplying it often and wear a hat.

The best clothing to wear for hiking are loose long pants, a shirt and good shoes, as opposed to shorts and sandals. A backpack may come in handy.

Be careful of loose rocks along the trail and of wet rocks, which may be slippery.

Insect protection may also be a good idea, especially if you plan to stop a while for a picnic lunch. Try not to disturb the small nests made by our local wasp, the Jack Spaniard, often found hanging from low-lying small branches.

Do not eat unknown fruits.

Do not climb on ruins. They are unstable and can collapse easily.

After or during a hike, you will probably want to take a swim, so it may be a good idea to bring along a swimsuit, a towel and a change of clothes.

Make sure that you are back before dark. The sun sets as early as 5:30 PM in winter and no later than 7:00 PM in summer.

Shorelines and guts
Knows your limits. Rock scrambling experience and good physical condition are essential for the Lind Point and Brown Bay shoreline hikes as well as for climbing up and down the Fish Bay and Battery guts. The Cocoloba and Reef Bay coastal walks are somewhat easier, but extreme caution is the rule.

Never attempt these scrambles alone. Let someone know of the group's hiking plan and the estimated time of return. Be especially careful climbing on wet or moss covered rocks which may be slippery.

Snorkeling safety
Always snorkel with a buddy.

The greatest danger to snorkelers is the proximity of boats. Use a dive flag to show your position. This is especially important in areas unprotected by swim buoys. Beware of breaking surf and currents.

Do not touch living coral.

Avoid sea urchins and fire coral.

Know your limits. Wear flotation devices if necessary.

Enjoy!
Proper precautions taken, relax. Enjoy yourself and have a good time.

section one

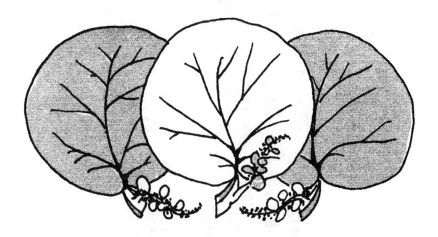

TRAILS

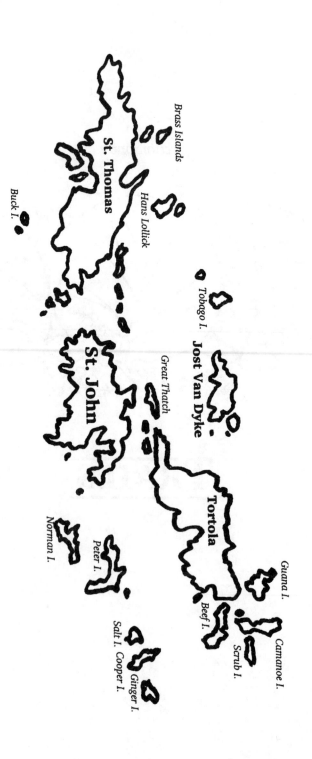

Brass Islands

St. Thomas

Hans Lollick

Buck I.

Tobago I.

Jost Van Dyke

Great Thatch

St. John

Tortola

Norman I.

Peter I.

Beef I.

Guana I.

Camanoe I.

Scrub I.

Salt I. Cooper I.

Ginger I.

THE LIND POINT TRAIL

The Lind Point Trail begins in Cruz Bay at the parking area behind the National Park Visitor Center and leads to the beaches at Salomon and Honeymoon Bays. The environment around the trail to Lind Point is cactus scrub. After that the setting changes to dry forest. There are moderate inclines that reach a maximum elevation of 160 feet. See Map 1, page 269.

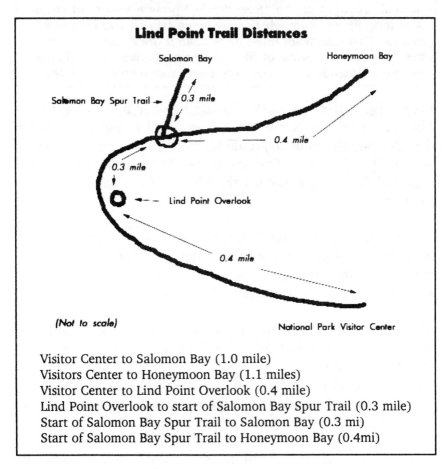

Visitor Center to Salomon Bay (1.0 mile)
Visitors Center to Honeymoon Bay (1.1 miles)
Visitor Center to Lind Point Overlook (0.4 mile)
Lind Point Overlook to start of Salomon Bay Spur Trail (0.3 mile)
Start of Salomon Bay Spur Trail to Salomon Bay (0.3 mi)
Start of Salomon Bay Spur Trail to Honeymoon Bay (0.4mi)

Although the trail passes through an area that was once devoted to cotton production, there is no longer any visible evidence of this industry.

American Cotton

Before the "discovery" of the New World, the only cotton available to Europe came from Africa. Since the fibers of this variety of cotton were too short for it to be woven, clothing was usually made from wool.

The Tainos, the people that the European explorers encountered on their voyages to the "New World," grew a variety of cotton with long fibers, from which they wove fabrics and made hammocks. This discovery must have been a great improvement in the European's quality of life, and now, thanks to the Tainos, people worldwide can enjoy soft, comfortable cotton clothing.

From the National Park Visitor Center to Lind Point

After about ten yards, the trail crosses a dirt road that follows the Cruz Bay shoreline to an old seaplane ramp that is no longer in use. The Lind Point Trail continues on the other side of this road and follows the eastern shoreline of Cruz Bay at a higher elevation.

The beginning of the trail is lined by the vine-like night blooming cereus. This plant produces a magnificent large white flower that blooms for one night a year. The flower then develops into a delicious fruit that tastes something like a kiwi.

After traveling about a quarter mile the trail forks near some large rocks. The main Lind Point Trail is to the right and goes uphill. The lower trail, which continues straight, runs parallel to the official Lind Point Trail, but at a lower elevation. Both trails access Salomon and Honeymoon Bays. The lower trail is slightly shorter and less hilly than the more scenic main trail.

The (upper) Lind Point Trail gains altitude through a series of switchbacks and then continues north toward Lind Point. This point, or headland, defines the northern extremity of Cruz Bay and the northwestern corner of the island of St. John.

At Lind Point, the trail forks, the left fork takes you to the Lind Point Battery Overlook, and the right fork continues to Solomon and Honeymoon beaches.

Cacti Found on St. John

Barrel Cactus
Barrel cactus is also called Turk's Cap Cactus, Pope's Head or Compass Plant (because they tend to tilt toward the south). They are round or barrel shaped and can grow in hard, rocky, windswept, and sun-drenched environments where little else can survive. The small pink fruit is edible.

Pipe Organ Cactus
This tall light green cactus branches at the base and has vertical stems. The spines grow in long rows and are extremely formidable. They can pierce clothing and light footwear such as sneakers or sandals. Some birds make their nests using the spines for support and protection against enemies. This cactus is also known in the Virgin Islands as Didildo Cactus or Dildo Cactus.

Prickly Pear
The prickly pear cactus has flat oval-shaped spiny pads. Yellow flowers grow from the edges of the pads that turn into a red fruit, which can be peeled and eaten.

The Lind Point Overlook

During the early nineteenth century the English found themselves at odds with the French who were then under the leadership of Napoleon. British fears were not confined to Europe. In the Caribbean the English faced the very real threat of a French takeover of St. Thomas and St. John, which would give France control of the strategic harbors of Charlotte Amalie on St. Thomas and Coral Bay on St. John. The British realized that by using the Danish West Indies as a base, the French would be in a strategically advantageous position in which to attack the British Virgin Islands and the rest of the British West Indies.

Fearing that the Danes would not be strong enough to defend their Caribbean territory against the French, Britain made a pre-emptive strike. British warships and soldiers were sent to St. Thomas and St. John with orders to take control of these Danish territories. Knowing that resistance was futile, the Danes surrendered without a single shot being fired and the French were effectively deterred from an easy takeover of the Danish islands.

In order to secure Cruz Bay harbor on St. John, the British built a fortification on Lind Point. The fort was hastily built and consisted simply of a semicircular platform supported by a well-built stone retaining wall upon which cannons were placed to defend the harbor.

The cannons are no longer there; only the stone wall remains. In their place is a wooden bench where you can sit and enjoy a view that juxtaposes unspoiled tropical scenery with the beginnings of modern development.

From Lind Point to Salomon and Honeymoon Bays

From Lind Point the trail turns right, or east, and follows the northwestern coastline.

The environment on this side of Lind Point changes to dry forest characterized by more and larger trees and broader leafed plants than the cactus scrub landscape on the other side of the point. Many of the rock formations along the hillsides are covered by epiphytes (air plants), such as bromeliads and anthuriums. What appear to be designs on the rocks, are caused by the growth of lichen.

A little more than a quarter mile from Lind Point the trail meets the quarter-mile trail to Salomon Bay. This trail will be on your left and goes downhill to the western end of the beach. This is the most common destination for travelers using the trail.

Anthuriums and Bromeliads

Anthuriums, and Bromeliads, like orchids and pinguins, are epiphytes, a nonparasitic plant that grows on another plant, but gets its nourishment from the air - thus, the name "air plant".

Anthuriums can grow on the ground, on rocks, or up in trees. The local varieties are Anthurium cordatum (heartleaf), Anthurium crenatum (scrub brush) and a hybrid of these two.

The heartleaf is more common in moist forest areas. It produces beautiful foliage that sometimes is home for tree snails and nests of wasps called Jack Spaniards.

The scrub brush anthurium has long green leaves with seasonal red fruit. The dried dead leaves have been used in the past to scrub pots and pans. They are just as effective as the commercial pot scrubbing products used today, plus they have the advantage of being easily disposable, non-rusting and biodegradable.

The heartleaf anthurium is common in the Lesser Antilles. The scrub brush anthurium is found in the Greater Antilles. They seem to have met on the islands of St. John and Tortola to produce a hybrid variety (anthurium selloum) which is only found on these two islands. It is sterile and cannot reproduce. The hybrid looks just like what you would expect a mixture of the two parent varieties to look like. See if you can identify one.

Bromeliads have long green serrated leaves and are similar in appearance to the pinguin or false pineapple, but not nearly as spiky. (See page 172 for information about the pinguin.)

For those not going to Salomon Bay, the Lind Point Trail continues straight ahead and runs on to Honeymoon Bay.

Before reaching the beach at Honeymoon Bay you will come to the intersection of the Caneel Hill Spur Trail and the Lind Point Trail. The Caneel Hill Spur Trail will be to your right and goes uphill. It is 0.8 mile long. This trail crosses the North Shore Road (Route 20) near the entrance to the National Park housing area and continues up the mountainside to an elevation of 300 feet where it meets the Caneel Hill Trail.

The continuation of the main Lind Point Trail will be to your left and goes downhill ending at an iron gate near a large tamarind tree. The gate serves to deter animals such as donkeys from entering the Caneel Bay Resort grounds. Pass through the gate and cross over the dirt road to get to the beach.

CANEEL AND MARGARET HILL TRAIL
CANEEL HILL ASCENT

The Caneel Hill Trail begins in Cruz Bay about twenty yards past the Mongoose Junction parking lot and rises to the summit of Caneel Hill. The trail then descends, running along the ridgeline to the saddle, or low point, between Caneel Hill and the next mountain peak, Margaret Hill. From the saddle the trail leads to the top of Margaret Hill and then goes down the opposite face of the mountain and arrives at the North Shore Road (Route 20) just across from the entrance to the Caneel Bay Resort. The total distance is 2.4 miles. See Map 1, page 269.

The trail to the peak of Caneel Hill is a steep and steady incline, gaining 719 feet of elevation in less than one mile. The view from the summit, however, is spectacular and well worth the fairly arduous climb to get there. Bring some refreshments, enjoy the cool breeze from the summit, and plan to stay a while to savor this unique mountaintop.

The Caneel Hill Trail passes through dry forest terrain in an area once dedicated to the cultivation of cotton. In the late nineteenth century the cotton plantations were sold or abandoned, and the land was then used primarily for pasture and for the cultivation of small provision garden plots until its acquisition by the National Park in the 1950s.

About a third of the way up the trail (0.3 mile) you will come to the intersection of the Caneel Hill Spur Trail, which will be to the left and leads downhill, crosses the North Shore Road, and then continues on to meet the Lind Point Trail. The trail to Caneel Hill is to the right and uphill.

A bench near the top of the trail will provide a welcome location to stop and rest and enjoy northerly views that are even better than can be seen on the summit.

At the peak of Caneel Hill you will be treated to a magnificent panorama. In 1995 Hurricane Marilyn destroyed the wooden viewing platform, but there is still a bench where you can sit and rest at the end of this strenuous climb. From this vantage point you can see a great deal of the Virgin Island archipelago and on clear days you may even be able to see as far as the mountainous El Yunque rainforest on Puerto Rico more than 40 miles west.

From Caneel Hill to the tamarind tree

From the summit of Caneel Hill the trail continues to the east and goes to the top of Margaret Hill. You will first make a rather steep descent down the eastern side of Caneel Hill. The track follows the southern side of the ridge between the two mountain peaks, and provides an excellent vantage point from which you can enjoy spectacular views of the southwestern side of St. John. The trail then crosses the crest of the ridge and runs along the northern side of the mountain opening up some views of the island's north shore and beyond.

The path continues to descend until it reaches the saddle (lowest point on the ridge) between Caneel and Margaret Hills where there is a large and ancient tamarind tree under which the National Park provides a rustic bench. This is an excellent place to stop for a rest and take advantage of the well-placed bench and the cooling the shade of this magnificent tree.

For details on the section of this trail that lies between the tamarind tree and the North Shore Road trailhead, see the next chapter, "The Caneel and Margaret Hill Trail - Margaret Hill Ascent."

CANEEL AND MARGARET HILL TRAIL
MARGARET HILL ASCENT

The 2.4-mile Caneel and Margaret Hill Trail begins (or ends) at the entrance to the Caneel Bay Resort on the opposite side of the North Shore Road (Route 20). The trail ascends 840 feet in the course of a little over one mile to reach the summit of Margaret Hill. From there it continues on to Caneel Hill and then down to Cruz Bay near the Mongoose Junction parking lot. See Map 1, page 269.

This is a highly recommended walk! The Margaret Hill ascent is shadier, cooler, and not as steep as the Caneel Hill ascent. As soon as you leave the paved roadway behind and enter the lush tropical forest, you cannot help but be overwhelmed by the serene natural beauty of the environment.

Notice the mottled bark of the commonly seen genip tree and the smooth and shiny trunks of the guavaberry and pepper cinnamon trees right at the beginning of the trail. There is also a lovely stand of teyer palms.

Teyer Palm

Some experts believe that the teyer palm is the only palm native to the Virgin Islands. Other horticulturists, however, insist that the royal palm is also a native species. In the not so distant past the teyer palm was used in St. John for making brooms and for strapping fish.

You will soon come to a stone wall, which lines one side of the trail. Growing along the wall are anthuriums and strangler figs.

The first National Park information sign you come to will direct you to the right and up. To the left are the remains of a now overgrown spur trail leading to a section of the Water Catchment Trail that is almost completely overgrown.

Strangler Fig (Clusia rosea)

The strangler fig is from the mangosteen family and is not a member of the fig family. It is also called autograph plant because, you can write on the leaves with a sharp pointed object. It can be used to leave messages or as playing cards. Another name for the tree is pitch apple because the sap from the bark and fruit was once used as caulking for wooden boats.

The strangler fig begins its life as an air plant usually in the fork of a host tree. It sends rapidly growing prop roots around its host to the ground. In time the numerous roots may strangle and kill the host tree. The strangler fig bears a white flower followed by a fruit that looks like a brown wooden apple. The fruit splits open in seven parts and then looks like a wooden flower.

As you gain elevation, views of the north shore and outer cays begin to open up through the foliage. This will be your signal to watch for a large approximately ten-foot tall triangular rock on the high side of the trail that is covered with beautiful native orchids.

Further up the trail are two separate spur trails both leading to the Water Catchment Trail, which at one time was a road used to connect the North Shore Road to Centerline via the Caneel Bay reservoir. It is now a walking trail, which runs between the Caneel and Margaret Hill Trail and Centerline Road.

Continuing along the Caneel and Margaret Hill Trail you will come to another large rock reminiscent of the orchid-covered one below. At this point the trail becomes rather steep and rocky and leads to a scenic overlook with a view to the north. It is only a few minute walk from this overlook to the top of Margaret Hill.

The Margaret Hill summit provides a fairly good view to the south, but the really spectacular overlook lies about fifty yards further down the trail marked by a National Park Service sign. Climb up on the large flat rock and enjoy!

***

Genip

The genip is commonly found along roadsides and trails. It is a member of the soapberry family and is a native of Venezuela and Colombia. These trees bear clusters of green fruit with a sweet edible pulp. Virgin Islanders are fond of ripe genips. They are often gathered and offered for sale by children or street vendors. The seeds can be roasted and eaten like nuts.

The genip tree has a distinctive smooth bark with a mottled gray green appearance. This effect is caused by lichen growing on the bark.

The leaves of the genip are believed to have insect repellent properties.

Guavaberry

The guavaberry tree is a member of the myrtle family. It has a smooth and shiny bark that is similar in appearance to the bay rum tree, but the leaves of the guavaberry are considerably smaller. The guavaberry fruit is either dark purple or yellow. It typically matures around September or October. The fruit is used to make pie, jams, and guavaberry wine, the traditional Virgin Island Christmas cheer.

Pepper Cinnamon

The pepper cinnamon has an extremely spicy smelling leaf. The bark peels off leaving a shiny trunk. The pepper cinnamon looks like the bay rum tree but has a yellow or cinnamon colored bark. Like bay rum and guavaberry, it is a member of the myrtle family. In South Florida it is called naked wood because of the peeling bark.

The pepper cinnamon is used medicinally to clear the sinuses by boiling the leaves in water and then inhaling the vapors.

Shortcut to the overlook

(If all you want to do is get to the Margaret Hill overlook and prefer not to take such a long hike, you can begin your walk at the entrance to the Water Catchment Trail at Centerline Road. Walk down to the spur trail. From there it is only a short walk to the overlook.)

The trail continues

From the Margaret Hill Overlook the trail continues to Caneel Hill and then runs back down to Cruz Bay near Mongoose Junction. For details on this section of the trail see the previous chapter, Caneel and Margaret Hill Trail - Caneel Hill Ascent.

TURTLE POINT TRAIL

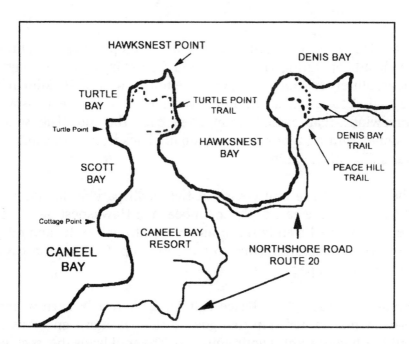

The Turtle Point Trail begins at the north end of the Caneel Bay Resort. Visitors should enter at the main gate and register at the front desk. This approximately half-mile trail is relatively flat, shady, and breezy and offers impressive views and diverse environments.

On your way to the Turtle Bay Trail entrance, be sure to enjoy the beautifully landscaped grounds and visit the impressive restored ruins dating back to the days of Danish colonization.

The trail begins at the eastern end of the Turtle Bay Beach and goes along the rocky shoreline around Hawksnest Point to Caneel Hawksnest Beach. There are benches along the way if you feel like stopping to enjoy the natural beauty all around you.

PEACE HILL AND DENIS BAY

Peace Hill is aptly named. Located on a hilltop at the end of the headland separating Hawksnest and Denis Bays you can enjoy an absolutely spectacular view of the north coast of St. John and beyond. Years ago a windmill was powered by the constant tradewinds that passed unimpeded over the hill. The semi-restored ruin now provides a dramatic backdrop to the unique tranquility of the hilltop.

The trail to Peace Hill begins at the small parking lot located about a half mile east of the main beach at Hawksnest Bay. This well maintained trail is short, about a tenth of a mile, and only involves a moderate incline to reach the top. See map on page 25 and Map 2, page 270.

About 20 yards up the Peace Hill Trail, there is a narrow and sparsely maintained trail that goes to the beach at Denis Bay. It will be on your right if your going up. The trail leads to a secluded section of beach on the western extreme of the bay. The little island that lies just offshore separated by a small stretch of shallow reef is called Perkins Cay.

History
Denis Bay was once a part of the Susanaberg Plantation, which was taken up by the Runnels family in the early eighteenth century.

Sugar works and settlements were established on both the upper (Susanaberg) and lower (Denis Bay) portions of the estate, which were connected by a road that descended the steep hillside by means of numerous switchbacks. This road still exists today, with some sections experiencing improvements, while other sections have been neglected to the point where the road is barely passable.

Denis Bay became a prosperous plantation and a good portion of the lower valley was either planted in sugarcane or devoted to pasture. A horsemill, and later a windmill, were constructed on top of Peace Hill. A long conduit brought the cane juice down to a boiling room near the beach where there was also an estate house, a warehouse, a rum distillery, and a slave village. These buildings have been partially restored and lie just behind the beach.

Sugar production at Denis Bay, and on St. John in general, began to decline in the mid-nineteenth century. By 1880 sugarcane was no longer grown at Denis Bay, and the property was used for provision farming and the grazing of sheep and cattle.

In 1877 Denis Bay, was split off from Susanaberg and in 1905 it was sold to J.E. Lindqvist, who began the operation of a small boarding house, known as Lindqvist's Place. At the time there was only one other such establishment in St. John, which was owned by Miss Myrah Keating and located in Cruz Bay.

Lindqvist also established a moderate sized garden at Denis Bay. Agricultural records for that period show that 2000 pineapples, 1000 banana plants and 500 coconut palms as well as some cotton and cocoa were cultivated on the Denis Bay Estate.

In the 1920s Denis bay was acquired by a group of St. Thomas businessmen who operated a sportfishing club called the Deep Sea Fishing Club. The club was available to the general public with hotel service and conveniences for $22.00 per week American plan.

In 1939 Julius and Cleome Wadsworth purchased Denis Bay.

Julius was a Foreign Service officer. Cleome was a professional fabric designer and worked in China and in Singapore, where she met Julius. They were married in 1932 and lived in Danszig, Prussia where Julius was serving as Consul. They came to St. John just before the outbreak of World War II in Europe.

The Wadsworths used Denis Bay as a vacation getaway. Their primary home since 1944 had been in Washington DC. Some illustrious St. Johnians have lived at Denis Bay either as renters or caretakers. Thomas Thomas served as one of the first caretakers and Robert and Nancy Gibney were some of the first renters having leased the property in 1947. The late Carl Frank, the founder of Holiday Homes was also a caretaker. He passed on the enviable job to Peter Griffith and family. One of the Griffith's daughters, Melanie Griffith, who became a famous actress, spent much of her childhood at Denis Bay.

Through a complicated series of real estate transactions the Denis Bay Estate is now the property of the Virgin Island National Park. Certain "remainder interests", which are the right to use a 1.1 acre parcel, containing the estate house, the warehouse and the old slave quarters will remain in private hands until 2035.

In the 1990s these "remainder interests" were sold to Ed Fine, son of the "Three Stooges" actor, Larry Fine. These rights have since been resold.

Cleome Wadsworth died on December 28, 1998 at the age of 102. Julius Wadsworth died in April of 1999. He was 96.

Peace Hill
In the 1950s the Wadsworths donated a seven-acre tract of land to the Virgin Islands National Park including the area known as Peace Hill, where the remains of the old windmill still stand.

The deed of gift to the park asserts:

> The grantors have for some years maintained Wadsworth's Peace Hill as a place where the public is invited to enjoy great beauty and quiet. It is their wish that Wadsworth's Peace Hill be perpetually dedicated as a place where people might meditate and find inner peace, in the hope that in some way this might contribute to world peace.

In 1953 Col. Wadsworth commissioned St. Johnians Terrence Powell and Thomas Thomas to construct the Christ of the Caribbean statue on the summit of Peace Hill. For many years this statue was a landmark for passengers and crews of vessels passing through the Durloe Channel who were treated to the dramatic spectacle of this likeness of Jesus Christ with outstretched arms looking out over the Atlantic waters with its implied message of peace and harmony.

In 1995 Hurricane Marilyn destroyed the Christ of the Caribbean which was, by this time, showing signs of decay. Even without the impressive statue, the summit of Peace Hill is a peaceful place to relax and enjoy the cool Atlantic breezes and magnificent vistas.

The dedication
When the Christ of the Caribbean statue was finally completed, Col. Wadsworth decided to christen it. He joined Terrence Powell and Thomas Thomas at the building site and produced a bottle of rum for this purpose. The colonel had forgotten his bible and went back to his house at Denis Bay to get it. The builders saw no reason to waste a good bottle of rum in this way. The rum was transferred to a different bottle and the monument was christened with what, some may say, was a more devout and more appropriate substance, seawater. (Story courtesy of Jimmy Powell)

CINNAMON BAY
SELF-GUIDING TRAIL

The Cinnamon Bay Self-Guiding Trail begins on the North Shore Road (Route 20) about ten yards east of the Cinnamon Bay Campground entrance on the opposite side of road. This level and shady half-mile loop trail, replete with National Park information signs, will take you through the remains of an old sugar and bay rum factory and then into the surrounding forest. See Map 2, page 270.

The Ruins

The twelve columns that at one time supported the factory storage room are plainly visible from the road, and this is an ideal place to begin the loop. This stone structure was used for the storage of crude brown sugar called muscavado, molasses, barrels of rum, and crushed and dried sugarcane stalks called bagasse, which were used for fuel and fertilizer.

South of the storage room are the remains of the horsemill and the boiling house. The sugarcane crushing apparatus was in the center of the horsemill and from there the cane juice flowed down the trough and into the boiling room. On the west side of the boiling room were the boiling trays where the cane juice was boiled down and transferred from copper pot to copper pot as it gradually thickened into sugar. The fires were stoked from the outside of the building. The large chimney still remains.

On the southwest corner of the sugar factory is the well-preserved bay rum distillery.

Bay Rum

The Danish West India Plantation Company acquired Cinnamon

Cinnamon Bay sugar and bay rum factory

Bay at the turn of the twentieth century. In 1903 they began growing fruit and bay rum trees for the production of the bay leaf oil, used in the popular cologne and lotion known as St. John Bay Rum.

Fruit cultivation did not turn out to be economically rewarding because of the difficulty in transporting the fruit to the European market. The fruits would often spoil before they could be sold.

Bay rum oil, on the other hand, showed some promise. It did not deteriorate rapidly and had the potential to be a profitable commodity. The success of this venture at Cinnamon Bay motivated other landowners on St. John to begin bay rum production.

Harvesting bay rum leaves was a labor-intensive process. Workers, who were often young children, had to climb the trees and carefully strip off the leaves. All the leaves could not be picked off the tree at one time, and neither could the leaves be picked more than twice a year to avoid damage to the tree. The leaves were put into large sacks and brought to the distillery. The harvester would only be paid eight cents for a 65-pound bag of leaves.

The forest trail

From the bay rum distillery the trail leads into the tropical forest and a magnificent stand of bay rum trees.

Bay Rum Tree (Pinenta racemosa)

The Bay Rum tree, also called cinnamon bay or cinnamon tree, is from the myrtle family. It has a shiny brown bark and dark green aromatic leaves. Many bay rum trees can be found in the Bordeaux Mountain and Cinnamon Bay area. Cinnamon Bay, originally called Caneel Bay, and Caneel Bay, originally called Klein Caneel Bay were named after the large bay rum trees found there. Caneel is the Dutch word for Cinnamon. Klein Caneel means Little Cinnamon.

The cemetery

A short spur trail to the left leads to an old Danish cemetery. Anna Margarethe Berner Hjardemaal, the wife of a former owner of the estate, is buried here in an above ground tomb. Her husband, Nicolai Severin Hjardemaal, a Dane, became the owner of Cinnamon Bay in 1834. The plantation was then called the America Hill Plantation. Hjardemaal's wife was born in St. Croix on November 7, 1785 and died at the age of fifty-one on November 27, 1836, just two years after she and her husband acquired the estate.

Slaves on the plantation were not afforded such an elaborate interment. They were buried at the beach at Cinnamon Bay. The erosion of the shoreline and heavy ground seas has caused the remains of some the deceased to wash out into the bay. Divers have reported finding skulls and other bones under rocks and coral around the western portion of the beach and at the next beach to the west, Little Cinnamon Bay.

Trees

After about a quarter mile, the trail crosses the gut. In this area you may notice several extremely large dead trees, some still standing and others which have already fallen. These trees were mammee apple trees. Up to about the early 1980s these magnificent trees lined the Cinnamon Bay portion of the North Shore road and grew in abundance in the forest near the gut. The mammee apple is native to tropical areas of the Americas. In the summer it bears a brown grapefruit sized fruit that was described by the Spanish chronicler Oviedo in the 1500s as "firmer and much better in taste than peaches". The die off may have been caused by a depletion of the underground water table in the 1980s when an unusual amount of water was taken from the wells.

In this area of the trail you can see the remains of the stone terraces that, in days gone by, were laboriously constructed by slave labor and planted with row after row of sugarcane.

A short distance after crossing the gut, the trail leads back in the opposite direction. The gut will now be on your right. Here is a small stand of cocoa trees, which grow a seedpod from which chocolate is derived.

Continuing along the trail, you will pass several large mango trees, which are hundreds of years old. These and other fruit trees were usually left standing when fields were cleared first for sugar cane production and later for cattle grazing and charcoal manufacture, and thus are some of the largest trees found on the island.

On this side of the gut are many guavaberry trees, which can be identified by their smooth shiny bark that looks much like the bay rum tree, but with smaller leaves.

The trail leads back to the estate house area of the plantation, and here you will find an excellent specimen of the distinctive calabash tree. The fruit of this tree, although not edible, is used to make bowls, purses and other handy items.

Estate house
The estate house is directly west of the sugar factory. In the early 1900s it was demolished by a hurricane. The house was rebuilt with the walls and roof made out of galvanized steel. The caretaker of the property lived here until the summer of 1969.

A cookhouse and oven are located west of the estate house. The oven was heated by burning coals or wood until the bricks became extremely hot. Then the ashes and remaining coals were swept out and the food was put in to bake.

Mongoose

According to *St. John on Foot and by Car,* by Randall S. Koladis, first written in 1974, the caretaker was known by natives "as a crafty old man who never lost a chicken to a greedy mongoose". He accomplished this by feeding his chickens a diet of coconut in the shell. He would break open the nut, but he never removed the coconut meat for them. The labor of separating the coconut meat from the shell gave the chickens a lot of exercise, and it kept them in good enough shape to outrun and out-maneuver the mongoose.

Mongoose

The mongoose was brought to St. John from India during the early Danish colonial period to control the rat population. Unfortunately rats are nocturnal and sleep in trees during the day. They were therefore able to eat as much sugar as they wanted by night, while the mongoose were sleeping, and the rats were safe, during the day, from the mongoose, which cannot climb trees.

The mongoose did have a great impact on other species, though. Mongooses sought out chickens and ground nesting birds and their eggs as well as turtle, lizard and iguana eggs. The rats meanwhile were free to eat not only the planter's sugar but also the eggs of tree nesting birds.

The mongoose became a nuisance for farmers and an environmental problem. This was officially recognized at least as early as 1936. In that year there was only one sign posted in all of St. John. It was nailed to the palm tree nearest the town dock in Cruz Bay. It was signed by the Government Secretary and embossed with the government seal. It announced a bounty, dead or alive, for mongooses, fifteen cents for a male and twenty-five cents for a female.

There is an old Virgin Island saying, Mongoose say, "If I had a cent, I would leave this island." Chicken say, "If I had a cent, I would lend it to you."

St. John Riddle...

W HAT is

THE PLURAL
OF
MONGOOSE

answer

mongoose dem

CINNAMON BAY TRAIL

The Cinnamon Bay Trail connects Cinnamon Bay with Centerline Road (Route 10). It begins about 20 yards east of the entrance to the Cinnamon Bay Campground on the North Shore Road (Route 20) just past the ruins, which are visible on the side of the road. This trail is 1.2 miles long and ascends steeply, gaining about 700 feet in altitude. See Map 2, page 270.

In the plantation days there was a rugged road going along the north shore of St. John between Brown Bay and what is now called Cinnamon Bay. To reach Cruz Bay from the north shore bays, such as Cinnamon, Trunk, Hawksnest, Denis and Caneel, it was necessary to first go up the mountain to Centerline Road (then called Konge Vey) and then head west from there. Most of these mountain routes were no more than horse or donkey trails. They generally followed the natural drainage guts in the mountain valleys. In areas where no trails had been cleared, the gut itself served as the path. The trail at Cinnamon Bay follows one of these Danish roads, which in the old days provided Cinnamon Bay with access to Konge Vey.

The beginning of the trail is the most difficult part, so don't be discouraged by the steepness and lack of shade. There is a conveniently placed flat rock near the top of the first steep ascent on the right side of the trail. It provides comfortable seating for two and may be a welcome rest stop. The trail soon levels off and crosses a gut. At this point you will find yourself in a relatively cool and shady forest. From here on, the ascent will be easier and shadier.

About 50 yards past the gut crossing is an old iron post that marks the beginning of the spur trail to the America Hill Estate

House. These remains of this old estate house are extremely unstable. (See America Hill Trail chapter, page 155.)

Continue up along the trail with the gut on your right. The forest is shady and cool with light filtering through the trees. There are many bay rum trees, and the air often takes on the aroma of the aromatic leaves.

Fruit trees
There are two large mango trees growing right beside the gut. Other fruit trees that you will pass on the trail are genip, guavaberry, tamarind, guava, mammee apple and hog plum. During most of the year, you will come across ripe fruits from at least one of these trees.

When you come to a fork in the trail, bear right. The other path soon ends in the bush.

Terraces
During the sugar plantation days most of this area was cleared and terraced by an enslaved labor force. The remains of these stone terraces are visible on the hillside above the trail.

Swales
Strategically placed along the trail are lines of rocks crossing at an angle. These serve to divert the flow of water across the trail and prevent erosion that would result from water flowing freely down the length of the trail. Some of these rudimentary culverts exist from the Danish days. This innovative management of the water run off kept many of the old Danish roads in fairly good condition for many years.

Charcoal
You will start to see a great deal of wild anthuriums growing near the trail. Off to the left, or upper side of the trail, try and

find a fairly well preserved terrace retained by a wall of dry stacked stones. In this area are the remains of a large hole where the earth appears to be black in places. This was once a charcoal pit.

Charcoal

Charcoal was an important industry during St. John's subsistence farming days. It served not only as the principle source of fuel for cooking, but also was sold for cash in St. Thomas. Charcoal was prepared by digging a large hole, then filling it with wood stacked in a triangle-like fashion. The wood was then layered with green grass, leaves and dirt. It was set on fire and left to burn for a week or two. This resulted in the production of St. John's fine charcoal which is still made today, although not very often.

Trees

After a series of switchbacks to gain elevation, the trail again crosses a gut. In this area you may find hog plum fruit when they are in season. The problem is that the hog plums are invariably too high to pick off the tree. Worms, birds and insects are usually quicker than hikers to find the ripe fruit that falls to the ground.

After another series of switchbacks, you will come to an area of tall beautiful trees, such as West Indian Locust, Kapok and Genip. You will pass under a natural bridge formed by a large tree that had at one time been forced down to a horizontal position. Despite the trauma, it continued its normal vertical growth pattern. This is a good example of geotropism, the tendency of plants to grow in a direction opposite the pull of gravity.

Overlooks

The path turns to the right and will bring you to two overlooks with splendid views. Looking west from the first overlook, you will see the island of St. Thomas in the distance, with Inner and

Outer Brass Cays offshore. You can look down the scenic channel formed by St. Thomas on one side and Thatch, Grassy, Mingo, Lovango and Congo Cays on the other. North of these cays you can see Hans Lollik and Little Hans Lollik. Looking down at St. John you have a lovely view of the valleys below. You can see large newly built houses at Peter Bay, down into the valleys fringed with coconut palms, and along the shorelines of Little Cinnamon and Cinnamon Bays. Cinnamon Cay and the shallow reef around its south side are visible a little offshore from the Cinnamon Bay campground. Out in the distance, north over the Cinnamon Bays, are the islands of Tobago and Little Tobago and Mercurious Rock. To the east, through the foliage, is Whistling Cay and beyond that White Bay on the Island of Jost Van Dyke.

At this overlook you will have the opportunity to see and identify some of St. John's exotic flora. The tree with the smooth and shiny bark is a guavaberry whose branches have provided a home for night blooming cereus, bromeliads and a termite nest. Also found at this overlook are a turpentine and both the scrub brush and heart leaf anthurium.

Turpentine Tree

The turpentine tree or gumbo-limbo gets its name from the turpentine-like smell of its resin. It is also called tourist nose tree because the reddish smooth bark continually sheds and can resemble the sunburned nose of a tourist. Another name for this tree is living fence post because branches could be cut and stuck into the ground where they will root and make a living fence.

Birds nesting in the turpentine tree are relatively safe from rats, because the rats have difficulty climbing the slippery bark.

The next overlook is about thirty yards up the trail and also offers spectacular views.

To Centerline Road

The trail continues upward through the forest until it emerges from the bush at Centerline Road. From here you can turn around and make the easier downhill hike back to Cinnamon or, if you have a lot of energy, proceed to the Reef Bay Trail, which begins about a mile down Centerline Road to the east (towards Coral Bay.)

FRANCIS BAY TRAIL

The Francis Bay Trail begins at the restored stone building at the intersection of the Leinster Bay Road and the Maho Bay Campground access road. It is a relatively easy 0.3-mile walk with only one small hill to negotiate. The trail goes through a dry scrub forest, past the ruins of an old residence and on to the beach at Francis Bay. It then winds through a mangrove forest and passes by a brackish pond before emerging from the mangroves at the dirt road between the beach entrance and the paved road at Mary's Creek. See Map 3 Page 271.

The renovated stone building at the beginning of the trail now serves as a National Park Service storage house. The two dates, 1814 and 1911, inscribed on the structure refer to the original completion and subsequent restoration of the building. There is a chimney attached to the structure with a hole in the bottom that leads to the inside of the storage house. Behind the storage building are old stone walls and other ruins dating back to the subsistence farming days on St. John.

The vegetation along the trail is disturbed and scrubby. This area was used to raise cattle for many years, and the land has not yet recovered.

Old residence

The ruins of an ornate old residence can be found on the right side of the trail about twenty yards from the trailhead. This structure is in unstable condition, and it is dangerous to get too close to or walk in the ruins.

There is a tile covered gallery floor, surrounded by a concrete railing that is still in fairly good condition. The house at one time

view from the balcony of former Mary Point residence

had a wood frame second story and the gallery was covered by a section of roof extending from the main building.

Unlike the traditional detached kitchens of the old Virgin Islands, the cookhouse for this residence was attached to the estate house. This kitchen boasted five ovens, which were placed under a stone hood leading to a chimney.

Stairs behind the cook house lead to another gallery above. Behind the gallery is a freshwater well, and to the west are the remains of another small structure.

Imagine a family living here in the not-so-distant past.

Bird Watching

Francis Bay is a favorite spot for bird watchers, and the National Park Service sometimes offers a guided bird watching walk along the trail. Two good places to observe the birds are, from above, at the pond overlook along the walking trail at the top of the hill and, from below, on the boardwalk that extends into the pond itself. Bring binoculars to fully enjoy these popular bird watching spots.

The following is taken from the article "Mary Point Pond, St John" by Jim Riddle, Robert Norton and Thelma Douglas appearing in Herbert A. Raffaele's authoritative book, *Birds of Puerto Rico and the Virgin Islands:*

> Nestled behind Mary Point, the northernmost point of St. John is one of the island's most productive birding spots. This pond, the nearby forest and the Francis Bay shoreline provide the observer with a great variety of birdlife at any time of the year. The brackish pond is rimmed by mangroves and other salt tolerant vegetation, which harbor migrants and local specialties such as Mangrove Cuckoo, Scaly-naped Pigeon, White-cheeked

Pintail and Smooth-billed Ani. There also are opportunities for good views of a variety of waterfowl, herons, shorebirds and warblers. Along the beach and rocky shoreline, Brown Booby, Brown Pelican, Magnificent Frigatebird and various terns can be seen offshore.

Francis Bay Beach and the salt pond

The path descends to the northern portion of Francis Bay Beach. At this point, you can go on to the beach or turn left to follow the trail along the edge of the salt pond. There are benches and a boardwalk on the banks of the salt pond from which this unique habitat can be comfortably observed. The trail continues alongside the pond until it emerges from the mangroves at the main road near the beach at Francis Bay.

Fruit trees

Several genip trees can be found along the walking trail and bordering the beach road. There are large tamarind trees just behind the sand at the northern end of the beach. Both varieties produce edible fruit. Enjoy them.

LEINSTER BAY ROAD

The Leinster Bay Road runs between the beach at Francis Bay and the Leinster Bay Trail. The distance between these points is about a half mile.

The mostly paved road hugs the coast of beautiful Leinster Bay where you will enjoy superb views from several places along the road.

The Leinster Bay Road accesses Francis Bay Beach, the entrance to the Maho Bay Campground, Francis Bay Trail, Mary Point School, Annaberg Sugar Mill and Leinster Bay Trail. See Maps 3 and 4, pages 271 and 272.

Manchineel
The low-lying coastal flatlands bordering the Leinster Bay Road are the habitat of the highly poisonous manchineel tree, one of which is marked by a National Park Service information sign. The sap from the leaves, bark or fruit of this tree can be irritating to the skin. Even standing under the tree in the rain can cause skin irritations. The round green fruit of this tree is also poisonous. On one of Columbus' voyages, a crewmember sampled the seemingly edible fruit and died. Thereafter, the fruit was nicknamed "death apple".

Bonefish
There are several places along the road where you can walk out to the narrow beach and observe the shallow reef flats. These reef tops are the habitat for wading birds, small fish and many species of marine invertebrates. The shallow areas called flats are also popular with fisherman testing their skills against the skittish and hard-fighting bonefish.

For runners

The Leinster Bay Road is one of the few long flat stretches on St. John. It is 0.7 mile long and is perfect for runners and joggers who prefer a level surface for their sport. If you begin and end your run at Francis Bay, you can enjoy the luxury of cooling off after your workout with a refreshing swim at one of the world's best beaches.

THE ANNABERG SCHOOL

The partially restored ruins of the Annaberg School, sometimes referred to as the Mary Point School, can be reached by means of a short (0.2 mile) well maintained trail, which begins off the North Shore Road (Route 20) about thirty yards from the intersection of the Leinster Bay Road. See map on page 165 and Map 3, page 271.

The National Park urges visitors to this site to be careful and to pay attention to road traffic when entering and exiting the trail.

The Annaberg School was one of the Caribbean's oldest public school houses. In 1987 the St. John Historical Society stabilized this site and provided an informational exhibit.

In 1839 the Danes passed a law requiring that both free and slave children attend school. The schools were built with funds obtained from the colonial treasury and were run by Moravian Missionaries. Classes were taught in English.

This concern for the education of the slaves was quite unusual considering the low priority given to schooling in the West Indian plantation societies in general. In the Danish West Indies public education, even for white children, was not available until 1788.

To justify the institution of slavery, the Europeans promoted a philosophy that Africans were somehow less than human and could not be educated. In most colonies education for Africans was prohibited either by law or by custom.

In the Danish West Indies this philosophy gradually became

more liberal. This was, in great part, due to the success of the Moravian Church in attracting African converts. White society now had to contend with the fact that many of these enslaved people were, like themselves, Christians.

Moravian clergymen taught the slaves at their missions in the islands, even before the passage of the 1839 law. They also pressed the government for educational reforms.

Another factor that led to the establishment of public schools for slave children was the ongoing process of humanitarianism and reform in Europe. King Frederick VI of Denmark was a liberal and a reformer. He maintained a friendship with Peter Van Scholten who was the governor of the Danish West Indies in the early 1830s. Van Scholten dedicated his governorship to the amelioration of the adverse conditions of slavery, and was instrumental in the passage of the educational reform law.

The Annaberg School was completed in 1844. The location was chosen because, at the time, this was the most populated area of St. John.

The recently renovated school building is representative of the architecture of the period. The location, overlooking Mary Point, Leinster Bay, and Tortola is quiet, serene and well worth a visit.

Use of the English language in the Virgin Islands

The official language of the United States Virgin Islands is English. At first this statement seems reasonable, as the language of the United States is English. Taking a closer look, however, we must remember that until 1917, the United States Virgin Islands had been a Danish colony for almost 250 years. Why then isn't the language of the Virgin Islands, Danish?

In fact Danish was never an important language in the Danish

West Indies. Denmark was a latecomer to the European practice of colonization. Lacking the military power of the other European colonizers, the Danes were only able to claim St. Thomas and later St. John, because no other European power really wanted these dry, rocky and hilly islands which were not particularly suited to sugar production.

Early explorers and settlers sent back tales of extreme hardship and rampant disease, and the Danes, who were generally comfortable at home, showed little interest in settling the new territories. Even an attempt to bring prisoners, promising freedom after six years labor, was met with riots, mutinies and other forms of resistance. As a result, the Danish government and its representative in the colonies, the Danish West India Company, resorted to inviting foreigners to settle the islands.

The majority of these settlers were Dutch. The African slaves working on the plantations were taught to speak a Dutch Creole, called Creolsk, and this became the common language of St. Thomas and St. John. The Moravian Church, which was influential because it ministered to the slaves, even translated the Bible into Dutch Creole so that the slaves would be able to understand it.

The question then becomes "Why isn't Dutch spoken in the Virgin Islands?"

The Danes purchased St. Croix from France in 1733. The most influential foreigners in St. Croix were English. In St. Croix English Creole was the dominant language and was spoken by most of the slaves. St. Croix had large areas of flat and fertile land. It received more rainfall than its neighbors to the north and was more suitable for a plantation economy. St. Croix's greater wealth and importance enabled it to exert a strong influence over the other islands of the Danish West Indies - St.

Thomas and St. John.

British occupation

In the early 1800s the Danish West Indies were occupied at two different times by the English, once in 1801 for almost a year and again from December 1807 until April 15, 1815. The purpose of the occupation was to secure the harbor at Charlotte Amalie and to prevent the use of the islands by the enemies of England. During this time more than 1500 English troops were stationed on St. Thomas and St. John further exposing the general population to British culture and the English language.

Publications

Newspapers, government proclamations and official documents began to be written in English. As a result, the use of English and English Creole became more and more widespread, not only in St. Croix, but also in St. Thomas and St. John.

Education

In 1839 the Danes passed a law requiring slave children to attend school. It was decided that the classes would be taught in English. This greatly accelerated the already established trend toward the common use of English in the Danish colonies and the Dutch Creole still spoken in St. Thomas and St. John was gradually phased out and is no longer spoken in these islands.

In the book *The West Indies and the Spanish Main*, Anthony Trollope made the following observation concerning St. Thomas in 1859:

> The people that one meets there forms as strange a collection as may perhaps be found anywhere. In the first place, all languages seem alike to them. One hears English, French, German and Spanish spoken all around one. And apparently it is indifferent which. The waiters seem to speak them all.

Charles E. Taylor in a description of St. John in the late nineteenth century wrote:

> Dutch Creole was once the prevailing language, many of the planters being of Dutch decent. The population which now numbers about 900, speak English.

Danish language in Africa

While the Danes were never successful in promoting the use of their language in their West Indian colonies, they did, however, have a great effect on their sphere of influence in Africa. Danish forts were established in the Accra area of the African coast in order to receive and process slaves bound for the Danish colonies. The Danes taught the Africans with whom they came in contact to speak Danish. This language is still spoken by many of the inhabitants of what is now the modern nation of Ghana and a significant amount of prominent citizens of Ghana have Danish names and relatives in Denmark.

The strong influence of British culture on these formerly Danish and now American islands answers yet another question commonly asked by visitors which is: "Why do Virgin Islanders drive on the left side of the road?"

ANNABERG SUGAR MILL

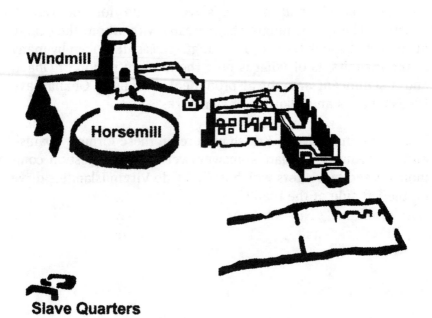

ANNABERG

The Virgin Islands National Park Service has prepared a self-guided tour of the historic Annaberg sugar mill ruins. The walk through this partially restored old sugar factory provides a great deal of insight to the history and culture of St. John during the plantation and post-emancipation eras. See Maps 3 and 4, pages 271 and 272.

Annaberg was named for Anna, the baby daughter of the absentee owner of the plantation, Christopher William Gottschalk. Translated from Danish, Annaberg means Anna's Hill. The plantation was first established in 1718.

Most of the Annaberg ruins that you see today were built in the nineteenth century. The wall of the horsemill and the slave house, however, date back to the eighteenth century.

Housing

The slave quarters (called worker's quarters after emancipation) barely remain. However, archaeologists have uncovered a wealth of artifacts here. There were more than 16 buildings in this area. They were made of daub and wattle. Wattle is a woven structure made of the wood from the false coffee bush. Daub is a type of mortar made of coral, lime and sand that were fired together and then mixed with molasses and mud. This mortar was packed into the wattle walls like plaster. The roofs were thatched with sugarcane leaves or palm fronds.

The Moravian missionary, C.G.A. Oldendorp, wrote a report on the progress of the Moravian Church in the Danish West Indies entitled, *A History of the Mission of the Evangelical Brethren,* published in 1777. In the following excerpt Oldendorp describes a typical slave dwelling:

> The layout and the foundation of their houses rest on four stakes, which are driven into the ground. Fork-shaped on the top end and shaped in such a manner as to form a square; these stakes are linked together at the top by an equal number of horizontal boards. On these rest the rafters of the roof which come together in a crest. A few more vertical stakes are placed between the corner posts, and pliable branches are woven among these. The latter are covered with quicklime and plastered with cow dung. Once the roof rafters have been covered with sugarcane leaves, the entire house is complete. The entryway is so low that a man can not pass through it without bending down. The doorway and a few small openings in the walls allow only a little light to flow into the dwelling during the day. The floor is the bare earth, and the two inclined sides of the roof, which extend almost down to the ground on the outside, make up the ceiling. An interior wall divides the house into two rooms of unequal size, the smaller one serving as a bedroom.

Sugarcane planting

As you walk through the ruins you will notice the steep hills behind the factory. This entire hillside was planted in sugarcane. First the land was slashed and burned. It was then terraced using the native stone as retaining walls. The cane was brought to the prepared fields and planted. Water had to be hauled to the sugarcane plants by hand. When it was time to harvest the cane, the slaves worked 18-20 hours a day. They cut the cane and loaded it into carts, which were drawn by donkeys to the sugar mill.

A typical day

The slave's day began at 4:00 a.m. when the bomba, or overseer, sounded the tutu (a conch shell with one end cut off). The slaves would get up and feed the livestock before reporting to work in the field at 5:00 a.m. They would work until the 8:00 a.m. break for rest and breakfast. Those slaves without food would eat sugarcane, when available. Work continued until noon. Between noon and 12:30 p.m. grass was gathered to feed the cattle. After the grass was collected there was an hour and a half break for lunch. Slaves with families would go home. Slaves without families generally stayed in the fields during the lunch break.

After lunch the slaves worked the fields until sunset. During the dead season, July to November, when there were no sugarcane crops, the animals were fed again, and the slaves could return home for the evening meal and the preparation of the next day's lunch. At times there would be additional work called "donker work". This was night work, such as hauling manure and water or cleaning up the master's yard. This work could last from about 7:00 to 10:00 p.m.

During crop time the workday was extended further, and women, and even the sick, were put to work cutting cane and bringing it to the mills.

The kaminas, or field slaves, were not given clothes by their masters, and many of them had to perform the laborious field-work naked in the heat of the tropical sun. They worked six days a week. On Sundays the slaves tended their garden plots called provision grounds. On some plantations the slaves were also allowed to tend their gardens on Saturday afternoon.

The windmill
On St. John, only the plantations at Annaberg, Carolina, Denis Bay, Susannaberg, Cathrineberg and Caneel Bay used windmills. The Annaberg windmill was built between 1810 and 1830. It is about forty feet tall. The wind powered blades turned the rollers that crushed the sugarcane. While the horsemill could only crush about 50 cartloads of cane per day, the more efficient windmill could crush 75-100 cartloads per day. The sugarcane had to be juiced within twenty-four hours of being harvested to prevent

spoilage. Slaves worked almost around the clock at harvest time. When it was windy both windmill and horsemill were operated simultaneously.

The Elaine Ione Sprauve Library and Museum in Cruz Bay has an excellent working model of a windmill. This is an extraordinary visual aid demonstrating the design and operation of the windmills used on St. John during the sugar era.

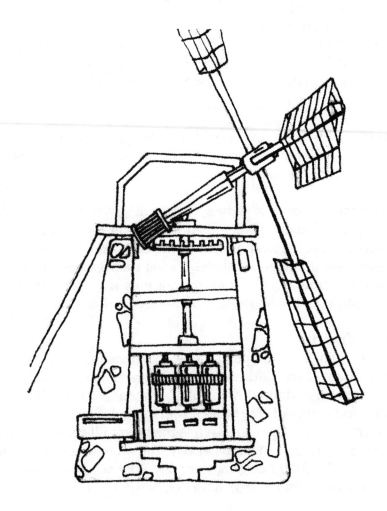

It took about ten slaves to work the windmill. Two of the men fed the bundles of sugarcane back and forth through the cane crushing rollers. An ax was kept nearby in case one of them got his hand caught in the rollers. If nearby workers acted fast enough, his arm would be chopped off before the rollers crushed his whole body.

When the horsemill was being used, horses, oxen or mules walked around the circular horsemill turning the three crushers. Four slaves were needed to run the animal mill. One drove the animals, two worked the rollers feeding the cane and one took away the left over sugarcane pulp called bagasse.

Sugar and rum production

The cane juice ran from the crushers down into the boiling room through wooden troughs. The bagasse was collected, dried, and taken to the storage shed. The cane juice then went into the first of five copper pots where it was boiled, using the bagasse as fuel for the fires. The thickened, boiled juice was then ladled into the neighboring pot and boiled to just the right consistency and then ladled into the succeeding pot. This was done, pot after pot, until a brown sugar, called muscavado, was produced. The workers in the boiling room had to be highly skilled. A mistake in timing would end up in the production of molasses, which was not nearly as valuable as sugar. The muscavado was then cooled and dried. The finished product was loaded into large wooden barrels called hogsheads containing about 1,000 pounds of sugar each. The barrels were brought to dories and then loaded onto larger vessels bound for Europe.

Rum was produced at the rum still. Sugarcane trash, cane juice drippings and molasses were fed into a fermentation cistern. The fermented liquid was then boiled in a copper still over a slow fire. The alcohol vapors rose up in copper coils that led into the cooling cistern.

The cool water of the cistern caused the vapor to condense, and a harsh raw rum called kill devil was formed. More refined rum was produced by aging the kill devil in wooden barrels for several years.

Water collection
Water was collected and stored in three cisterns, which were all connected by aqueducts. One cistern is located within the ruins at the mill. The remains of the others are higher up on the hill.

The provision ground
The Danish colonization of St. John was characterized by the establishment of a plantation economy dedicated to the production of sugar, cotton and other tropical products. Africans, forced into slavery, provided the labor for these plantations. Under such a system the slave owner had to decide how the slaves would be fed.

Ideally (for the slave owner) food would be brought in from outside the plantation, giving the slave owner complete control of his captives. This was not practical on St. John plantations, which were, at best, only marginally successful. The cost would have been too high for the owners to bear.

Another possibility would be to produce food on the plantation itself, under the supervision and control of the slave owner. On St. John, however, cleared and terraced land came at too high a cost in time and labor to be devoted to food crops.

On the other hand, St. John plantations did have a great deal of land on the periphery of the cultivated areas that, although not suitable for sugarcane production, was appropriate for food crop cultivation. This was the plantation owners' solution for feeding their slaves.

Thus, the slaves produced their own food, unsupervised by the slave masters, on garden plots called provision grounds located on the less productive areas of the plantation and tended these gardens when they were not working elsewhere on the estate.

The slaves were absolutely dependent on their ability to produce their own food. Statistics show that the slave population suffered significant declines after periods of prolonged drought indicating that many slaves must have died when they could not produce sufficient food to feed themselves.

Statistics also show an increase in marooning (slaves running away from their plantations) during prolonged dry spells. A severe drought in the early 1730s was one of the principal causes of the St. John slave rebellion. The drought was so long and so severe that there was widespread starvation among the slaves. Their situation was so desperate that many left the plantations to live in the bush as maroons, despite laws, which prescribed severe and horrible punishments for this offence. An armed insurrection followed in 1733.

After a long drought in the 1770s there were again reports of large population declines and as a result of the starvation caused by the failure of the slave's provision grounds, sixty slaves made the difficult and dangerous decision to run away from the Estate Carolina plantation in Coral Bay.

Although the additional responsibility of providing for their own food was a great hardship for the already overworked slaves, the system did provide the slaves with certain hidden benefits.

Because the provision grounds were unsupervised, the slaves were able to gather and interact out of the sight of their masters. Although often forbidden, slaves from different plantations could meet on the more remote provision grounds. On these occasions cultural traditions could be passed on, news could be disseminated, and conspiracies involving escape and resistance plans could be discussed.

Slaves often worked together on their plots and shared the harvest. Those who were strong and healthy supported the old, weak or infirm. On some plantations the slaves were able to produce a surplus of food, charcoal or crafts and a system of exchange developed along with an underground economy, which even provided some slaves with enough money to buy their freedom.

Moreover, the tradition of an agriculturally based society enabled the slaves to survive on St. John after the failure of the sugar industry and the end of slavery.

A tradition of independence, extended family, cooperation and sharing developed around the provision ground. This spirit is still evident on St. John even in these modern times, which tend to be more orientated toward individualism and self-interest.

Grand maroonage (escape by sea)
During the years that slavery was abolished in the British Virgin Islands, but continued in the Danish West Indies (1840-1848), the proximity of St. John to Tortola provided a temptation for slaves seeking freedom. Tortola was just across the Sir Francis Drake Channel from Annaberg. In May of 1840, eleven slaves escaped from Annaberg and Leinster Bay to Tortola. This was the first major escape of slaves during the period following emancipation in the British Virgin Islands.

After emancipation
Slavery was abolished in the Danish West Indies in 1848. Planters on St. John tried to keep the slaves working on the plantation by the use of labor laws designed to perpetuate the

plantation system. Slaves, now known as workers, could not leave the plantations. Wages were kept artificially low and often were paid in the form of goods called an allowance.

After emancipation, slavery continued on St. John in practice, if not in theory. Other factors, besides legal proclamations, eventually ended this unofficial system of slavery. The price of sugar declined with increased competition from other areas that were better suited to produce sugar than the dry, rocky and steep hills of St. John. The sugar beet was introduced, putting further pressure on the industry. In addition, disgruntled workers began to offer resistance to the unjust labor laws. They brought their grievances to the Danish authorities, organized strikes and work stoppages, and often ran away to Tortola or St. Thomas.

In 1867 a major hurricane, followed by an earthquake, led to the abandonment of Annaberg by the owner. Two hundred laborers on the Annaberg and Leinster Bay Plantations were left to fend for themselves. They asked the authorities' permission to stay on and work the plantations on their own but were refused.

The twentieth century
The cookhouse at Annaberg was built in the early 20th Century by Carl Emanuel Francis. Food was baked in iron pots called coal pots. Charcoal was placed underneath the coal pot, which was then covered with galvanized steel. Additional charcoal could be placed on top.

Herbs for medicine and cooking were gathered from the bush or grown in the garden. Maran bush was used for brooms and pot scrubbing (it scrubbed and deodorized as well). Sea fans were used as a whisks and sifters. Baskets were made from hoop vine.

Mr. Francis also built a house on the site of the horsemill. It was rebuilt after the great hurricane in 1924. The family survived by taking refuge in the windmill, which, although it had no roof, provided the necessary protection. (St. John did not experience another major hurricane until Hurricane Hugo in 1989.)

Francis raised cattle on the estate from the early 1900s to about 1935. In 1935 Mr. Francis sold Annaberg to Herman Creque who left it to his wife Emily. In 1955 Annaberg was sold to the Rockefeller controlled Jackson Hole Preserve Inc. and donated to the National Park. When the National Park acquired the land in the 1950s, they dismantled the house. The cookhouse is all that remains.

LEINSTER BAY TRAIL

The Leinster Bay Trail is a flat 0.8-mile trail that follows the shoreline of Leinster Bay from the end of the paved road beyond the Annaberg parking lot to the beach at Waterlemon Bay. The Johnny Horn Trail begins just behind the beach and continues on to Coral Bay. See Map 4 Page 272.

The Leinster Bay Trail is a particularly beautiful walk as it leads right along the water's edge offering splendid and unobstructed views of Leinster Bay, the Narrows, Sir Francis Drake Channel, and West End, Tortola. Moreover, it provides land access to one of St. John's best snorkeling locations, Waterlemon Cay, the small island that lies just offshore of the beautiful little beach at Waterlemon Bay. (For snorkeling details see page 235.)

The beach

In 1918 Luther K. Zabriskie offered the following description of Leinster Bay in his book, *The United States Virgin Islands*: "Smith Bay [Leinster Bay] with its fine bathing beach can not be easily forgotten. The bottom of the bay is of beautiful white sand spread like a carpet."

Waterlemon Cay

The small island of Waterlemon Cay once served as an arena for settling disputes and matters of honor. The Danes had outlawed dueling and as a result, hot-blooded men from St. Thomas and St. John would go to Tortola where dueling was legal. In 1800 the British Virgin Islands also prohibited dueling. The remote and uninhabited island of Waterlemon Cay, far from the eyes of the Danish authorities, became the new "field of honor."

Before Hurricane Marilyn in 1995, the Leinster Bay Trail was passable by four-wheel drive vehicle. According to the National

Park the decision not to repair the road to a condition that would once again allow vehicle entry was made in order to lessen the impact on the reef at Waterlemon Cay by snorkelers arriving by vehicle.

The Leinster Bay Trail was once part of the Old Danish Road that began in Coral Bay and followed the north shore of St. John accessing the plantations at Brown Bay, Leinster Bay, Annaberg, Mary Point, Fredriksdal, Windberg, Little Maho Bay and Caneel Bay (Cinnamon Bay). Today, this route consists of the Brown Bay Trail, Johnny Horn Trail, Leinster Bay Trail, Leinster Bay Road, and the North Shore Road (Route 20) as far as Cinnamon Bay.

The ruins

Behind the beach at Waterlemon Bay are the extensive remains of the Leinster Bay Plantation as well as what is left of a more recent cattle operation. There is a great deal of thorny cassia and catch-and-keep so wear long pants and good shoes to explore here, and be sure to move about cautiously.

Just inland of the Johnny Horn Trail entrance are the remains of a small residence. Further back in the bush is an old well tower. If you look in, you will see water at the bottom. There are three more wells on the site. One well is near the brackish pond, and two more are in the valley.

Just past the well are the ruins of the storage house, the boiling room and the boiling bench where sugarcane juice was boiled down to produce crystallized sugar. Here you will see smooth black limestone tiles that look like slate. These tiles, made in Denmark's Gotlin Island in the Baltic Sea, are often found around the burning trenches of old sugar mills.

The ruins of the horsemill are behind the boiling room. Also remaining on this old estate are the gatepost, the rum still and the canning room.

Archeologists have found evidence of at least twenty-six slave houses on the hillside to the east of the plantation.

History of Leinster Bay

Jan Loison took up the plantation at Leinster Bay in 1721. He was a French refugee, who came to the Danish West Indies as a result of the revocation of the Edict of Mann, which had previously protected the Protestants known as Huguenots against persecution.

Loison, unlike many plantation owners of the time, did live on the property. He married a woman named Maria Thoma. Jan Loison died in 1724 just three years after starting up the plantation. The widow Maria married Lt. Peter Froling who was the commander of Frederiksvaern, the fort in Coral Bay. Peter Froling was one of the characters in the historical novel by John Anderson, *The Night of the Silent Drums*.

According to old tax records, by 1728 the plantation was growing sugarcane, and within a year a sugar works had been established. The estate was 2,650 feet long and 1,500 feet wide. (They were taxed by the width of the parcel, and this was usually the smaller measurement.) There were six capable slaves (slaves who had either been born into slavery or had adjusted to the routine), one bussal slave (a slave brought directly from Africa) and two manquin slaves (slaves who had physical disabilities).

The plantation was destroyed in the slave rebellion of 1733-1734.

Karen Fog Olwig in her book, *Cultural Adaptation and Resistance on St. John,* University of Florida Press, Gainesville, FL 1985, writes about an incident that occurred on the Leinster Bay Plantation in the early nineteenth century. It offers this histori-cal insight concerning one of the methods of resistance employed by St. John slaves:

> In 1818 at Leinsterbay Plantation a slave was punished so severely that he died as a result. Forty-seven slaves subse-quently ran away and hid in the bush. Officials came to the plantation and tried to make the slaves go back to work. They were stoned and forced to flee. It took a force of thirty soldiers sent by the governor to end this rebellion.

In 1822 Hans Berg, a prominent and wealthy Dane and former governor of the Danish West Indies purchased Leinster Bay. Berg also owned the Annaberg Plantation and several estates on St. Thomas.

In 1863 Thomas Lloyd became the owner of the Leinster Bay Plantation, as well as the Annaberg estate. In October of 1867 there was a devastating hurricane which was followed about ten days later by a severe earthquake. Most of the remaining sugar plantations on St. John ceased to operate after that. Leinster Bay and Annaberg were devastated by the twin disasters.

Lloyd gave up any hope of restoring the property and left for Tortola without making any provisions for the future of the plan-tation or the workers. He left two hundred employees with no means of support whatsoever.

After emancipation in the Danish islands, the former slaves became employees. Their status, however, was not much better than it was under slavery. The laborers asked the authorities if they could stay on and work the plantation on their own. The complexity of the labor laws left them in a state of limbo. They could not leave the island without a passport and permission, nor could they simply leave and work elsewhere. Furthermore, the authorities refused to let them farm the abandoned estate. This incident, however, helped to point out, and eventually change, these archaic laws which were designed to maintain the plantation system and keep the former slaves tied to their estates.

In 1874 George Francis bought Leinster Bay after he returned from the Dominican Republic. He died shortly thereafter, and his widow sold it to the Danish policeman Henry Clen, who married a member of the Francis family.

In 1914 a man named Jorgeson bought Leinster Bay, and in 1920 it was sold to Herbert E. Lockhart of the prominent St. Thomas Lockhart family. He owned the estate until 1972, when it was acquired by the United States Government as part of the National Park.

The Lockharts used the property for cattle production. Members of the Samuels family from Coral Bay looked after the estate and the cattle for Lockhart. When it was sold to the National Park, the Lockharts abandoned the remaining cattle.

JOHNNY HORN TRAIL

The Johnny Horn Trail connects the Leinster Bay Trail at the eastern end of the beach at Waterlemon Bay with the historic Emmaus Moravian Church in Coral Bay. The trail is 1.8 miles long and follows the mountain ridge through a dry upland forest environment. There are some steep hills reaching an approximate elevation of 400 feet.

There are four spur trails off the main trail. The first (starting from Waterlemon Bay) provides access to the best place to cross the channel if you would like to snorkel around Waterlemon Cay. The second spur leads to the remains of an old Danish guardhouse. The third trail takes you to the ruins at Windy Hill, and the fourth is the Brown Bay Trail to Brown Bay and East End. See Maps 4 and 5, pages 272 and 273.

The name
The Johnny Horn Trail was named after Johan Horn who was second in command to Governor Gardelin in St. Thomas and Commandant of St. John around the time of the slave rebellion in 1733. He was the Chief Bookkeeper and Chief Merchant of the Danish West India and Guinea Company on St. Thomas. According to John Anderson in his historical novel *Night of the Silent Drums*, Englishman John Charles, a former actor who became a small planter on St. John, said the following of Horn:

> He had a grimace for a face, lies for eyes, noes for a nose, arse cheeks for face cheeks, fears for ears, whips for lips, dung for a tongue, and to all who knew him it seems strange that he has but one horn for a name.

Snorkeling access spur trail
Right near the beginning of the Johnny Horn Trail there is a short

spur trail that follows the shoreline of Waterlemon Bay. By walk-ing along this trail you can get to a point on the shore that is half the distance to Waterlemon Cay than it would be starting from the beach. This way you can save your energy for the really good snorkeling around the cay.

Genip tree

There is a genip tree about fifty yards up the trail, just before the turn off to the guardhouse. Some of these trees produce sweet-er fruit than others. This is a good one! Keep an eye out for ripe genips in the summer.

Aloe

A patch of aloes can be found a little further up the trail between a big rock and the remains of the old Guardhouse. People often planted these medicinal plants, used for the treatment of sun-burn, burns and other ailments, close to homes and public build-ings.

The guardhouse

The spur trail on the left, just beyond the aloes, takes you to the ruins of a Danish guardhouse. This small fortification was built on this strategic location, called Leinster Point, because it over-looked two critical passages, the Fungi Passage, between Whistling Cay and Mary Point, and the Narrows, which separate Great Thatch and St. John. The guardhouse was equipped with cannons and manned by sixteen soldiers.

Great escapes

Slavery was abolished in the British Virgin Islands on August 1, 1834. By the complicated terms of the law all slaves less than six years of age were to be freed immediately. House slaves had to complete a four-year "apprenticeship" and field slaves a six-year "apprenticeship" before they received full emancipation. By 1840 all the inhabitants of Tortola were free, while in nearby St.

John the institution of slavery was to continue until 1848. British law granted free status to anyone who arrived in their territory. These factors created a situation whereby slavery and freedom were only separated by a mile and a half of water.

The channel between St. John and Tortola, although narrow, is generally characterized by rough seas and strong currents. Nonetheless many St. John slaves braved this crossing in whatever manner that was available to them. Some arranged with friends or relatives in Tortola to meet them in some secluded bay and take them across. Others stole boats or secretly constructed rafts out of whatever material they could find including estate house doors. Some brave and hardy souls even swam across the treacherous channel.

The first major escape from St. John occurred in May of 1840 when eleven slaves from the Annaberg and Leinster Bay plantations fled to Tortola. This event was followed a week later by the successful escape of four slaves from the Brown Bay Plantation.

The guardhouse at Leinster Point was built in order to prevent more of these escapes. Another stone structure, which can still be seen on Whistling Cay, was also utilized to prevent slave escapes. In addition to guardhouses, cannons, and soldiers on the land, Danish naval frigates patrolled the waters. The captains and crews of these vessels were ordered: "shoot to kill."

One night in the year 1840 five slaves left St. John's north shore in a canoe. A Danish naval ship spotted them somewhere in the western Sir Francis Drake Channel, between St. John and Tortola. The soldiers opened fire and a woman was killed. The others jumped into the sea. Another woman and a child were apprehended and returned to St. John, but the remaining two fugitives got away by swimming the rest of the way to Tortola. The story of their ordeal created an international incident.

The line separating St. John from Tortola was no more defined in 1840 than it is today. The government in Tortola protested the killing of the woman in what appeared to be British waters. The protest led to an official investigation of the occurrence and the court martial in Copenhagen of a Lieutenant Hedemann for the murder of the woman and the violation of British territory. The lieutenant was found guilty and was sentenced to a two-month prison term.

The St. John slaves had an underground network of contacts in Tortola who often aided in their escapes. On the night of November 15, 1845 thirty-seven St. John slaves secretly left their plantations and assembled at a deserted bay on the sparsely inhabited south side of St. John. While the Danish Navy was busily patrolling the north shore of St. John, the 37 men and women, safely and without incident, boarded the vessels and were transported to a new life in Tortola.

Between the years 1840 and 1848 more than 100 St. John slaves were able to find freedom in the British colonies.

Windy Hill

As you proceed up the hill you will come to several areas that provide excellent views to the north. Near the top, the trail forks. The spur trail to the left leads to the ruins of an estate called Windy Hill. The trail to the right is the continuation of the main Johnny Horn Trail.

The Windy Hill ruins are about 200 yards down the left spur trail. The structure was originally built as the estate house for the plantation and sugar works at Leinster Bay. In 1843 it was owned by Judge H. Berg, the vice-governor of the Danish West Indies. Berg, who lived in St. Thomas, was also the owner of the Annaberg Plantation at that time.

When he visited St. John, he would reside at Windy Hill. Otherwise, the house was occupied and managed by a Mr. and Mrs. Wallace. Preserved letters from early travelers to St. John make reference to the presence of an extensive library at Windy Hill.

Before selling the remainder of his estates on St. John, Judge Berg bequeathed small plots of land east of the estate house to some of his employees. These employees and their descendants established the village of Johnny Horn. Remains of the old houses can be seen in several places just off the Johnny Horn Trail.

Luther K. Zabriskie, in his book, *The United States Virgin Islands*, gives this description of Windy Hill when it was a boarding house:

> Leinster Bay, was where an excellent boarding house, for use by occasional visitors, was once kept. The storm of 1916 blew this house down. The wonderful old mahogany furniture that was the envy of all who came to stay here, was scattered in all directions.

Windy Hill may also have been used as a Masonic Lodge. De Booy and Faris in, *Our New Possessions*, wrote:

> Near by are the remains of a building occupied by the only Masonic Lodge on St. John. One can almost picture the banquets held by the Masons when they assembled here in the olden days, when feasts were of the first importance in the life of the West Indian planter.

From *The Langford Mail*:

> Windy Hill was the private boardhouse of a Mrs. Clin (commonly spelled "Clen"). It was owned by lawyer Jorgenson and entirely destroyed in hurricane of 1916.

In 1917 when the United States bought the Virgin Islands, a reform school was established here. Mrs. Clen was in charge of the facility. Most of what you see now is from that period.

Brown Bay Trail
Following the relatively flat ridge you will find scenic overlooks with views of Jost Van Dyke, West End, Tortola, and the Sir Francis Drake Channel. About a half mile from the Windy Hill spur, you will come to another trail intersection.

The Johnny Horn Trail continues straight ahead and the Brown Bay Trail is on the left. It is identified by a National Park information sign.

The Brown Bay Trail is 1.6 miles long. It is 0.8 mile to the beach at Brown Bay and another 0.8 mile to the East End Road at the other end of the trail. See chapters on Brown Bay, pages 77 and 239.

Brown Bay spur to the Moravian Church
Continuing straight along the Johnny Horn Trail the path descends gradually and crosses a gut. After crossing the gut, the trail ascends steeply before reaching a more improved section of dirt road near the summit of Base Hill (pronounced Boss Hill). At this point you will have reached an altitude of 400 feet above sea level, from which there are superb views down into Coral Harbor and Coral Bay. The road descends rapidly and leads to the Moravian Church in Coral Bay near the intersection of Centerline Road (Route 10) and Salt Pond Road (Route 107). The church, constructed in 1919, is listed in the National Registry of Historic Sites.

The Moravians came to St. John in 1741. They established the mission at Emmaus (Coral Bay) in 1782. They are the oldest of the Protestant religions and were the first to minister to blacks. This is the fourth Moravian church to be built on this site.

BROWN BAY TRAIL

The Brown Bay Trail runs between the East End Road (Route 10) just east of Estate Zootenvaal, and the Johnny Horn Trail. The beach at Brown Bay is 0.8 mile from either end of the trail making a total distance of 1.6 miles. See Maps 4 and 5, pages 272 and 273.

From East End to the beach at Brown Bay

If your destination is the beach at Brown Bay, the easier access is from the trail entrance at East End. Starting from the Coral Bay Moravian Church, go east about a mile on the East End Road. You will pass Estate Zootenvaal and then cross a small concrete bridge. Turn left just after the bridge and park on the dirt road. An animal watering trough and an old well remaining from subsistence farming days can be found on the low flat ground on the west side of the trail near the road. Twenty yards up the dirt track you will come to a fork in the road. The right fork is the beginning of the Brown Bay Trail.

This section of the Brown Bay Trail will take you from the south side of St. John, up a hill, over the ridge and down to the north side of the island. At the ridge you will have reached an altitude of 200 feet above sea level.

As you walk along the trail you will quite likely encounter feral donkeys and small herds of goats that roam freely through the bush.

On the south side of the hill you will see pipe organ cactus, century plants, maran bush, catch-and-keep and wild tamarind, which are characteristic of this cactus scrub environment. Among the larger trees found in the vicinity are tamarinds and genips, which usually bear fruit in the summer months.

Be careful not to step on the cacti that lie low on the ground and are known locally as suckers. The spines can be quite painful and hard to dislodge if you get stuck.

There is a fine southerly view of Coral Bay just before the trail switches back to the right for the first time. You can look out over Coral Harbor, Princess Bay, Hurricane Hole and Leduck Island.

Crossing over the top of the ridge you'll begin your descent into the Brown Bay Valley. The north side of St. John typically gets more rain than the south side resulting in a thicker coverage of trees and a more tropical environment, a phenomenon you will quickly notice as you cross from one side of the mountain to the other.

As you descend into the valley you will be treated to beautiful views of the Sir Francis Drake Channel and the bordering British Virgin Islands

At the bottom of the hill, take the short spur trail to get to the beach at Brown Bay or continue on the same trail that will intersect with the Johnny Horn Trail.

The Johnny Horn Trail to the beach at Brown Bay - an alternate approach

If you are beginning this walk from the Johnny Horn Trail, proceed to the intersection of the Johnny Horn and Brown Bay Trails. The Brown Bay Trail is to the left and goes downhill.

About 20 yards from the intersection is a scenic overlook. On a clear day there is an excellent view to the east all the way to the Baths at Virgin Gorda, including Fallen Jerusalem, Round Rock, and Cooper and Salt Islands.

At the bottom of the hill the trail crosses a gut and continues east on flat land. At the gut crossing there are several genip trees and a large tamarind tree. Donkeys and goats often congregate around this area.

The trail passes alongside a salt pond for about a quarter mile. A little past the salt pond is a short spur trail to the left that leads to the beach at Brown Bay. The Brown Bay Trail continues to East End Road, just east of Estate Zootenvaal.

For beach and snorkeling information on Brown Bay, please refer to the chapter entitled, "Brown Bay", page 239.

The ruins
Brown Bay has some of the most extensive ruins on the island of St. John. To explore them proceed to the western end of the beach and then make your way further along the shoreline until you see the beginning of the ruins.

Here you will find the remains of an estate house bearing an old concrete plaque inscribed with the date 1872 and bearing the initials "G-N". Notice the exceptionally well-crafted stone and brickwork that went into the construction of the old walls. You will also find ruins from an even earlier time including a sugar factory with its boiling room, cisterns once used for rum distillation, an old copper boiling pot, two horsemills from different periods, a storage building, an old well, an ox pound and two graves, one being that of a child.

Slavery and Brown Bay
When French troops finally put down the slave rebellion of 1733, surviving slaves gathered above Brown Bay and shot themselves dead rather than face capture. This occurred about

10 days after the mass suicide at Ram Head.

Slavery was abolished in the British Virgin Islands eight years before the emancipation of slaves in the Danish islands in 1848. During this time many St. John slaves took advantage of the proximity of British Tortola to attempt an escape to freedom. One of the first recorded incidences of these escapes occurred in 1840 when it was reported that four slaves from the Brown Bay plantation successfully escaped across the channel to Tortola.

Wild Tamarind (Leucaena leucocephala)
Wild tamarind, or tan tan, was brought to St. John around 1820 and has proven to be quite prolific. It grows wherever land has been disturbed. Although many gardeners and landscapers hate this scrubby tree, the wild tamarind does have some redeeming characteristics. It is nitrogen fixing plant, which means that it can take nitrogen out of the air and turn it into compounds that enrich the soil. It also has a deep tap root system, which is effective against erosion. The wild tamarind wood has also been used in charcoal production and to feed goats. Horses and donkeys are not fed wild tamarind because it can make them go bald.

Catch-and-keep (Acacia riparia)
Riparia is a good name for the thorny vine that tends to rip your clothes when you walk past it. Catch-and-keep has sharp barbed hooked spines on its stem and leaves that can readily catch onto clothing or skin and be reluctant to let go, catching you and keeping you caught.

Maran Bush (Croton discolor)
Maran is a weed-like bush that is found in the drier parts of the island especially in areas that were once used for grazing. Maran is poisonous to cattle, and they refuse to eat it. They will eat almost everything else, so the maran has less competition in grazed areas and becomes the dominant species. Virgin Islanders used maran leaves as a pot scrubber. They are coarse enough to remove burned-on food and have a sage-like odor that serves as a deodorizer. Moreover, maran leaves are completely biodegradable and, unlike steel wool pads, they are non-rusting.

REEF BAY TRAIL

The April 1996 Tenth Anniversary Collectors Edition of <u>Caribbean Travel and Life</u> magazine chose St. John's Reef Bay Trail as one of the Caribbean's 10 best hikes.

The Reef Bay Trail begins at Centerline Road 4.9 miles east of Cruz Bay. Parking for four or five vehicles is available opposite the trail entrance. The trail runs between Centerline Road and the ruins of the Reef Bay sugar factory near the beach at Genti Bay. The well-maintained 2.4-mile trail descends 937 feet from the road to the floor of the Reef Bay Valley. The average hiking time is two hours downhill from Centerline Road to the beach. See Map 8, page 276.

Planning the hike

The National Park Service offers guided hikes down the Reef Bay Trail. Transportation is provided from the National Park Visitors Center in Cruz Bay to the head of the trail. An experienced park ranger will act as your guide. In addition to the Reef Bay Trail, the walk will include the spur trail to the petroglyphs and a visit to the Reef Bay sugar mill. From the beach near the mill, you will be met by a boat, which will take you back to Cruz Bay, allowing you to avoid the more strenuous walk back up the trail. This popular activity is offered for a modest fee by reservation only.

Those making their own arrangements for this hike need to consider their transportation to the trailhead on Centerline Road and the method of return from the bottom of the trail.

The simplest procedure is to leave your vehicle in the parking area across from the trailhead on Centerline Road, walk down the trail, and then walk back up the way you came. No formal arrangements have to be made; you can go whenever you want, with whomever you want. However, the long, steep, uphill walk back is far more difficult than the descent. This should not be a problem for those in good physical condition who may even enjoy the challenge. Make sure to pace yourself and bring plenty of water. It may also be a good idea to plan a picnic either at the petroglyphs or at the beach near the sugar factory. A cooling swim at Genti or Little Reef Bay is another pleasant way to prepare for the walk up the valley.

By arranging transportation on both ends of the trip, or by being prepared to hitchhike, it is possible to exit the Reef Bay Valley without having to go back up the way you came.

One method is to take the Lameshur Bay Trail from the Reef Bay Trail to Lameshur Bay. This involves backtracking about a mile from the Reef Bay sugar factory to reach the trail, then walking 1.5 miles with a rapid 467-foot altitude gain, and subsequent descent in order to reach the road at Lameshur Bay. This is not much easier than returning uphill on the Reef Bay Trail, and it is only recommended for those in good physical condition. It will be necessary to pace yourself and to bring water. See the chapter on the Lameshur Bay Trail, page 109 for trail details.

Another alternative is to walk along the coast to the western end of the bay where there is access to a road in Estate Fish Bay. Transportation should be arranged on both sides of this hike, as it is a long way back to the trailhead, and hitchhiking is difficult on the infrequently traveled roads of Fish Bay. For more information on this walk see the chapter entitled "Reef Bay Coastal Walk" page 134 and Map 9 page 277.

The geography of the Reef Bay Valley
Webster's Dictionary defines a valley as "an elongated depression between uplands, hills or mountains, especially one following the course of a stream." In this sense the Reef Bay Valley,

located on the south side of St. John is a classic example of this geographical formation.

The steep and well-defined mountains that form the Reef Bay Valley are among the highest in St. John and the valley follows the course of two streambeds, locally called guts. The Reef Bay Gut begins at Mamey Mountain and runs down the center of the valley to Reef Bay. Parallel to the Reef Bay Gut on the western side of the valley is the Living Gut, also called the Rustenberg Gut, which begins near Centerline Road and meets the Reef Bay Gut at the lower levels of the valley. A freshwater pool formed by the Living Gut provides the location of the ancient Taino rock carvings, which we call the petroglyphs.

The history of the valley

The first human inhabitants of Reef Bay were hunter-gatherers who arrived in St. John almost 3,000 years ago. These primitive peoples were conquered or replaced by a farming oriented society who were the biological ancestors of the Tainos, the people who Columbus encountered on his voyage across the Atlantic. The farmers, like the hunter-gatherers migrated from the South American mainland and up the island chain of the Lesser Antilles arriving in St. John about 2,000 years ago.

When Columbus sailed past St. John in 1493 he reported the island to be uninhabited. The Tainos that lived on St. John may have already fled the island in the wake of Carib raids or they may have gone into hiding at the approach of Columbus' fleet, later to fall victim to the depredations visited upon them by the Spanish colonizers. In the early sixteenth century St. John was reported to be re-inhabited by Amerindians fleeing Spanish persecution in St. Croix and Puerto Rico. By 1550 the island appeared to have been totally uninhabited, and it remained that way for about 100 years.

Between 1671 and 1717 St. John was intermittently occupied by small groups of European woodcutters, sailors, fisherman and farmers.

St. John was officially colonized and settled by the Danes in 1718. By 1726 all of the land in the Reef Bay Valley had been parceled out to form 12 plantations. At first these estates were devoted to a variety of agricultural endeavors such as cotton, cocoa, coffee, ground provisions (yams, yucca, sweet potato taro, corn, etc.) and the raising of stock animals as well as to the production of sugarcane. By the later part of the eighteenth century the twelve plantations were consolidated into five, and sugar became the dominant crop in the valley. Only Little Reef Bay never switched to sugar. They grew some cotton but primarily concentrated on ground provisions and animals that were sold to the neighboring plantations.

Although much of the land was cleared for agricultural purposes, a large portion of the valley was left in its natural state. The least disturbed areas of the valley are the western side of the Reef Bay Gut and the mountain spur between White Point and Bordeaux Peak.

By the end of the eighteenth century, when sugar production was at its peak, and the population of the valley was at its greatest (300), about half of Reef Bay Valley was classified as woodland.

In the nineteenth century, agriculture in the Reef Bay Valley began to decline. By 1915 only Par Force and Little Reef Bay in the lower valley were still active, but with only 10 acres planted in sugar. Otherwise the plantations were devoted to cattle and other livestock, coconuts, fruit trees, and ground provisions.

Today most of the Reef Bay Valley, with the exception of some parcels of private property called "inholdings" is the property of the National Park.

From Centerline Road to Josie Gut
The Reef Bay Trail begins at the bottom of the stone stairway on the southern side of Centerline Road.

Looking up toward Centerline Road from the bottom of the stairs you can see an old stone wall. This was once the retaining wall for the circular horsemill on the plantation known as Old Works and is all that remains of the old estate, which was demolished during the construction of Centerline Road.

The Reef Bay Trail roughly follows the course of the Reef Bay Gut. The top section of the trail descends steeply through the moist sub-tropical forest of Reef Bay's upper valley where there is an abundance of large trees, such as locust, sandbox, kapok, mammee apple and mango. National Park information signs along the way will provide valuable information about the natural environment of the valley.

Josie Gut Plantation
The ruins of the Josie Gut Sugar Estate can be found about a half mile down the trail. The plantation began operation in the early eighteenth century. The circular horsemill, supported by an old stone retaining wall, is still in good condition. A small storage room was built into the lower portion of the retaining wall. The boiling room, now in a state of ruin, lies right below the horsemill, just a few yards off the trail.

Construction materials
The walls and foundations of the structures found at Josie Gut were constructed using locally obtained stone, brain coral, and imported red and yellow bricks. These bricks, made in England and Germany, can be found in the ruins all over the island. The

Josie Gut Plantation

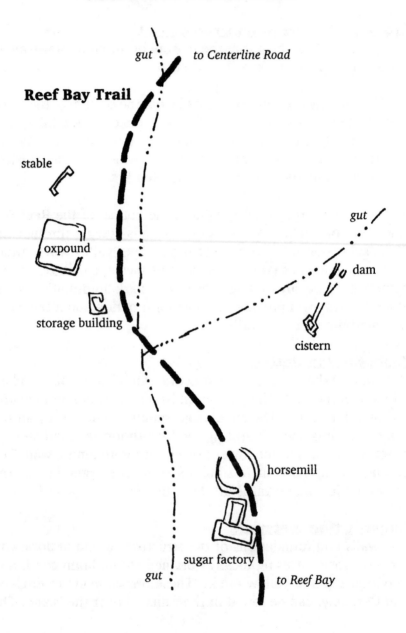

gut · · to Centerline Road

Reef Bay Trail

stable

oxpound

gut ·

dam

storage building

cistern

horsemill

sugar factory

gut · ·

to Reef Bay

story of how they ended up in the walls of a Caribbean sugar plantation provides some insight into the culture and morality of the time and place from which they came.

During the plantation days the traditional trade route to the West Indies was called the triangle trade.

The first leg of the triangle trade was from Europe to Africa. The ships carried rum, weapons, and manufactured goods that were offloaded in Africa and traded for slaves.

The second leg of the trade was from Africa to the West Indies in which the holds of the ships were crowded with a human cargo, slave labor for the plantations in the New World.

Sailing vessels need weight, called ballast, toward the lowest sections of the ship to balance the force of the wind on the sails. This is accomplished today by the use of heavy keels or lead weights loaded near the bottom of the hull area.

The simple fact that dead or dying human beings could not be sold motivated the slavers to make certain efforts to keep their property in a sellable condition. In order to further this goal, the Africans captives were moved on deck from time to time to get fresh air and to enable the crew to wash down the accumulated filth below. In short, the human cargo was not suitable as ballast, and some other weighty material needed to be in place in the lowest sections of the hull.

Preferably, the ballast would be easily removable when the ship reached the West Indies in order to make room for the hogsheads of sugar, barrels of rum, bales of cotton, and other tropical products that would fetch a handsome price in Europe. European bricks were often chosen to serve as this ballast material. Not only were they compact and heavy, but they also had value in the West Indies where they could be sold as construction material.

Brain coral was another important construction material. It was used primarily on arches and as corner stones. Brain coral served this purpose well because when it is first brought from the sea, it is soft and can be cut easily with a saw to the size and shape needed. After the brain coral was shaped it would be placed in the sun to dry where it would become hard and rock-like.

Stone, already plentiful on the surface of the ground, was also uncovered during excavations for terraces, buildings and roads.

Mortar was made from a mixture of lime, seashells, water and molasses. The lime was fabricated locally by burning chunks of coral and seashells.

The framework and roofs of the buildings were made of wood. Many of the larger beams were made of the extremely hard and durable lignum vitae, a tree that was once plentiful on St. John.

From Josie Gut to the sea

After leaving the Josie Gut area the trail becomes less steep and the environment gradually changes to a dry forest, characterized by smaller trees and sparser shrubbery.

About one mile from Centerline Road, now well within the more gently sloped lower valley, the Reef Bay Trail passes by the remains of a small house, which was built around1930. This section of the Reef Bay Valley is known as Estate Par Force. The house alongside the trail was once owned by Miss Anna Marsh, who cultivated fruit trees and raised cattle.

In those days permission had to be granted by Miss Marsh in order to continue down the trail to the abandoned sugar mill or to the petroglyphs.

From St. John Backtime, *Hands and Hours are Never Enough,* by Erva Boulon, July 17, 1934:

> Erva Claire, Anne, Jack Jean and I started out this A.M. with our lunch and three donkeys. We went up to Hammer Farm, (Herman Farm or Cathrineberg) turned off onto Centerline and turned down the trail to Reef Bay. We stopped at Miss Anna Marsh's place and asked to go up to the pools. We followed the river bed along and saw all the pools, stopped and made a fire and ate our lunch and then went a little farther....We started back about one, went to Miss Marsh's and she gave us coconuts. They were so good...

Also from *St. John Backtime,* "Not a Wheeled Vehicle on the Island" by John E. Jennings, 1938:

> ...At Reef Bay is a well preserved old house, set high on the hillside, and the ruin of an elaborate old sugar mill. Both of these are the property of a fine old Negress named Miss Marsh, who lives in a rickety shack near the mill. Miss Marsh is inclined to be a little mite suspicious of visitors, and seems rather cranky at first. However if she takes a liking to you she will thaw noticeably after the first few words of conversation and will probably end by offering you coconut juice direct from fresh green coconuts whose ends have been chopped off with a machete. Miss Marsh is one of the few natives of St. John who has been to New York. When asked how she liked it, she proved herself a discerning woman by replying: Oh, bless God, not for me...

In 1938 Miss Marsh was murdered and her gold ring was stolen. The murderer was apprehended when he attempted to sell the ring in St. Thomas.

Estate Par Force

About twenty yards down the main trail from the Anna Marsh house ruins there is a narrow trail leading to the ruins of the Par

Estate Par Force

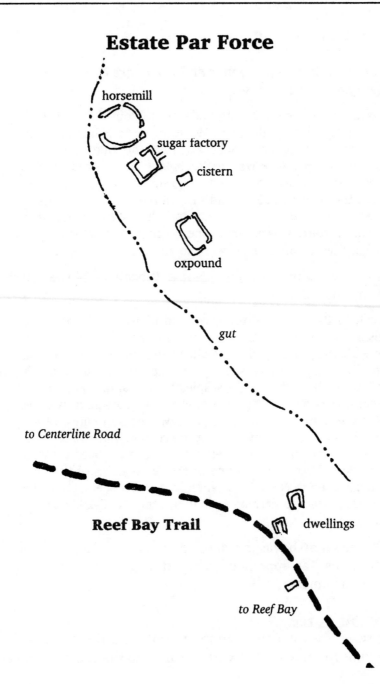

horsemill

sugar factory

cistern

oxpound

gut

to Centerline Road

Reef Bay Trail

dwellings

to Reef Bay

Force Estate and continuing up to the Reef Bay Estate House trail. Since Hurricane Marilyn, however, this trail has become practically impassable. A visit to the Par Force Estate ruins can still be reached from the other end of the trail at its intersection with the Reef Bay Great House spur trail. This trail is not maintained and not easily negotiated.

The Par Force Plantation was parceled out in four separate sections between 1721 and 1724. By 1765 the four estates were reconsolidated into one plantation again called Par Force.

In 1830 John Vetters bought the Par Force property as well as Estate Little Reef Bay on the coast. Vetters had a new sugar factory built near the beach at Genti Bay and the old sugar mill complex at Par Force was abandoned.

A new estate house was built in 1832 and reconstructed in 1844. In 1994 the estate house was partially renovated by the National Park.

The combination of land, including the new estate house, became known as Estate Reef Bay and was owned by the Marsh family until the 1950s when the land was acquired by the Virgin Island National Park.

From Par Force to Genti Bay
About 0.1 mile past the Anna Marsh house you will come to the intersection of the Lameshur Bay Trail. This trail leads to the left (east) while the Reef Bay Trail continues straight. For information on the Lameshur Bay Trail see page 109.

The next trail intersection, which comes right after the Lameshur Bay Trail, is the Petroglyph Trail, which will be on your right, (heading west).

The Reef Bay Trail continues straight (south) on relatively flat terrain and leads to the partially restored Reef Bay sugar factory and the beach at Genti Bay.

Many citrus trees were planted along this section of the Reef Bay Trail, and some lime trees still remain. Two of these trees are growing right alongside the trail. If you find ripe limes, take a few back with you. They're especially delicious and make excellent limeade.

In her book, *Some True Tales and Legends About Caneel Bay, Trunk Bay and a Hundred and One Other Places on St. John,* Charlotte Dean Stark remembers collecting fruit in Reef Bay:

> There are cultivated orange trees there (at Estate Reef Bay), and once, to our joy, in 1948 or 1949, there was enough rain to produce a crop of five hundred oranges. They were exceptionally sweet and of fine flavor.

As the trail nears the sea it passes through a low-lying marshy area. The holes in the earth are land crab holes. This was once a popular place to gather these island delicacies. Land crabs are now protected within the National Park boundaries and hunting them is forbidden.

William Henry Marsh

In 1855 O.J. Bergeest and Company bought Reef Bay and converted the mill to steam power. At that time, William Henry Marsh was the manager of the plantation. Marsh had come to the West Indies from England along with his brother. They both settled for a time in Antigua. William went to live in Tortola and then moved to St. John. His brother settled in New York.

William Marsh was in charge of setting up the steam engine. In 1864 he bought the entire Reef Bay Estate at public auction. He married a St. Johnian and had 10 children. The Marsh family acquired several other estates on St. John, and they are, to this day, important landowners on the island.

The turn of the twentieth century

Around the turn of the twentieth century the Par Force or Reef Bay Plantation operation covered almost the entire lower part of the valley. Sugar was planted just north and east of the factory behind the marshy area. The provision grounds were planted at the northern end of the valley just before it starts to slope steeply upwards. Another provision ground was located next to the great house. Coconut palms and bananas were cultivated in the lower area near the beach. Fruit and citrus trees were planted throughout the lower valley, but especially near the gut. Cattle and sheep grazed on three sections set aside as grassland.

The Reef Bay sugar factory

The Reef Bay sugar mill remains in extremely good condition. A visit here may increase your understanding of the sugar making process and help you to imagine what life was like in days gone by.

A good way to start your tour of the factory is to begin at the horsemill. Horses, mules or oxen walked in continuous circles to power the three rollers of the cane crusher in the center of the mill. A slave (or after 1848, a "worker") on one side of the crusher fed bundles of cane into the rollers, and a slave on the other side would receive them. He, in turn, would send the crushed stalks back through the rollers for further extraction of the cane juice.

The cane juice then flowed down the trough to the boiling room. The leftover crushed cane stalks, called bagasse, were dried out and stored.

One side of the boiling room housed the boiling bench and the

horsemill

row of copper boiling pots where the cane juice would be boiled down into a wet raw sugar called muscavado. The fires were fed from the outside of the building. Bagasse would often be burned to provide heat for the boiling operation. The muscavado would then be dried and packed into 1,000 pound barrels called hogsheads.

Sailing vessels bound for Europe would arrive in Genti Bay to pick up the shipments of sugar. To accomplish this, specially constructed boats called dories were used to bring the hogsheads to the larger vessel. The dory would be beached and then turned on its side. The heavy barrels would then be rolled inside. Then the dory would be righted, launched and rowed out to the anchored vessel. Using block and tackle on the boom of the sailboat, the sugar could then be loaded into the cargo area below decks.

Reef Bay Sugar Factory

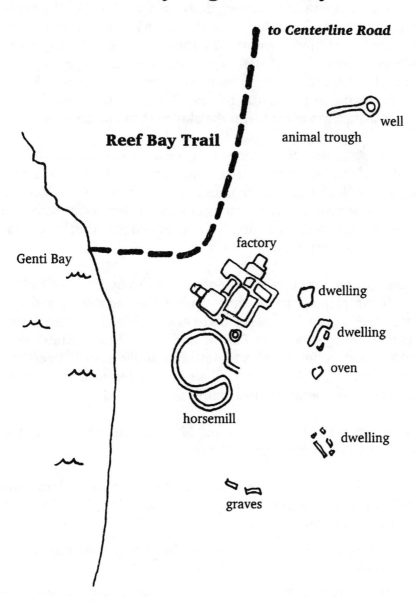

Steam power

After the abolition of slavery in the Danish West Indies, the sugar industry on St. John began to collapse. Most of the sugar plantations on St. John were sold, and their new owners switched to cattle raising or provision farming. The owners of Reef Bay, however, decided to continue the sugar operation. To make the process more economically feasible, they installed a steam engine to power the rollers. This, they felt, would solve the problems associated with the slowness of animal power.

At the perimeter of the horsemill, next to one of the factory walls, is the steam powered sugarcane crusher. The steam engine, built in Glasgow Scotland in 1861 by the W.A. McOnie Co., is located in the room alongside the rollers. This room was constructed especially to house the steam engine after it was put together and installed.

The sugar operation here did not proceed smoothly. The soil on the sugar plantations became depleted of nutrients, and the sugar crops became smaller and smaller. Moreover, the introduction of sugar beets in Europe and in the United States provided great competition and lowered sugar prices. Reef Bay Estate and Estate Adrian, which also converted to steam power, were the last operating sugar mills on the island.

On March 7, 1908 fifteen year old Maunie Dalmida was crushed in the gear assembly next to the rollers.

The following account is taken from research done by Lito Valls and Ruth Hull Low in the book, *St. John Backtime*, "Boy That Got Caught in the Cogs":

> The undersigned was sent at Par Force to get information regard to a boy that got in the cogs of the mill.
>
> The east part of the boiling house has a passage 3.5 feets wide

in that is the cogs, a large one connect to a small one which is 3.5 feets from the ground. The boy Dalmida and James Samuel was there thrown up canes to Eban Thamas the distant from Dalmida to J. Samuel was 6 feet distant. With his back toward Dalmida, J Samuel hord the craking, he then look bahind him saw Dalmida in the cogs. Mr. Marsh (E.W. Marsh, the son of W. H. Marsh) was outside of the boiling house, he run and stop the ingin. He was all redy broken in too. The right hand was also smash, the belly was smash, his bowels was torn asunder. Eben Thamas was 7.5 feet off and did not see.

I have summung these party to meet on Monday at 1 Ocl.(o'clock).

Mr. E.W. Marsh, James Samuel, Eben Thamas.

E.W. Marsh, the son of W.H. Marsh, died a year later and left the property to his four children, two of whom stayed on to run the plantation. The sugar operation became even more difficult after the accident because some people believed that the mill was haunted by ghosts.

In 1916 St. John was struck by a major hurricane. The factory was closed and the sugar era on St. John finally came to an end.

By 1930 only five people lived in the Reef Bay Valley at Par Force. They tended two acres of provisions and grazed 44 cattle. The estate was then owned by Anna Marsh, the daughter of William Henry Marsh, who sold small amounts of milk, citrus fruits, guavas, mangos and coconuts.

Reef Bay remained sparsely occupied until the early 1950s.

In 1955 much of Reef Bay was sold to the Rockefeller's Jackson Hole Preserve Inc., which donated the land to the National Park.

The grave of W.H. Marsh
Behind the horsemill, about twenty yards inland from the beach,

is the well preserved above ground grave of W.H. Marsh. His two daughters are buried nearby.

Historical bathrooms

An item of somewhat esoteric historical interest is the origin of the bathrooms located near the beach. The former island administrator and park ranger, Noble Samuels, took Ladybird Johnson on the Reef Bay Hike in the early 1960s.

Upon reaching the sugar factory at the end of the trail, the former First Lady asked Noble Samuels for the location of the bathrooms. The park ranger acknowledged the lack of these facilities and pointed to the bush as a possible alternative.

Ladybird Johnson later donated money for the construction of the bathrooms which are there for your convenience today.

PETROGLYPH TRAIL

In the lower section of the Reef Bay valley there is a freshwater pool surrounded by large, smooth rocks. It is fed by a waterfall that cascades down a 40-foot cliff where strangler figs and wild orchids have taken root using cracks and crevices in the rock face as footholds.

The pool provides an environment for shrimp, frogs, small fish, dragonflies and hummingbirds, and at night bats zip back and forth attracted to the sweet water. The vegetation is lush and tropical and the ambiance is serene and tranquil. There is an air of magic and spirituality here that undoubtedly inspired previous inhabitants of St. John to carve drawings and symbols into the rocks surrounding the pool. We call these rock carvings the petroglyphs.

If you're coming down the Reef Bay Trail from Centerline Road the Petroglyph Trail will head off to your right at a point 1.6 miles from trailhead. Coming up from the sugar mill it is 0.8 miles to the Petroglyph Trail, which will be on your left.

From the intersection of the two trails it only requires an easy half-mile walk over flat terrain in order to reach the petroglyphs. See Map 8, page 276.

There are several theories on the origin of the petroglyphs, but none can be absolutely proven. Apparently, there is not yet a reliable scientific method for dating the carvings.

The most popular (and most plausible) theory attributes the petroglyphs to the pre-Columbian inhabitants of St. John.

Reef Bay was a settlement site for a wave of pre-ceramic hunters and gatherers that came up the island chain of the Lesser Antilles and arrived on St. John about 3,000 years ago.

Around the time of Jesus Christ a new group of migrants arrived on St. John. They were a more advanced society of farmers and artisans who worked with clay and fabricated distinctive pottery. They also originated on the South American mainland and migrated throughout the Lesser Antilles and on to the Virgin Islands and Puerto Rico. With the arrival of the newcomers the previous inhabitants of these islands were absorbed into the new society, killed or driven off.

When they reached Hispaniola, however, the newly arrived immigrants came into contact with an ancient people who were the very first human beings to occupy the islands of the West Indies. This group of pre-ceramic hunters and gatherers were strong enough to halt the advance of the farmers, and for the next few hundred years the two societies faced each other off in the region of the Mona Passage between western Puerto Rico and eastern Hispaniola.

The interaction of the two cultures eventually gave rise to the great Taino nation that spread westward throughout Hispaniola, Jamaica, Cuba, and the Bahamas, and eastward into Puerto Rico and the Virgin Islands.

Archeological evidence, especially the dig at Cinnamon Bay, proves conclusively that the Taino and their ancestors once lived on St. John. Moreover, a characteristic of Taino society was their propensity to carve pictographs around freshwater pools, along streams and rivers, on rocks found in caves, on coastlines, and at ceremonial sites such as ball courts. Petroglyphs similar to the ones at Reef Bay have been found at other former Taino settlements in Puerto Rico, Hispaniola and on various other islands throughout the West Indies.

Archeologist Ken Wild points to a bat motif found on many Taino artifacts, and historians have learned from the writings of the early Spanish chroniclers, who met the Taino, that the bat was an important religious symbol. Furthermore, what appears to be bat noses on a human faces can be seen on some petroglyphs. An interesting concept is the fact that petroglyphs are often found in areas frequented by bats such as water sources and caves. The petroglyph pool on St. John is one of these places. At night the sky over the pool is full of bats that come there to get water.

Given the overwhelming historical and archeological evidence, the vast majority of archeologists, historians, anthropologists and ethnologists have concluded that it was the Tainos who carved the petroglyphs in Reef Bay.

However, there are other theories.

One hypothesis is that Africans carved the petroglyphs. In 1971 the visiting ambassador from Ghana noticed a striking similarity of one of the pictographs to an Ashanti symbol that means, "accept God".

Going further afield is the research of the eminent cryptographer, Dr. Barry Fell, who identifies the petroglyphs as being similar to "the Tifinag branch of a medieval Libyan script ... used by multi-racial peoples in South East Libya as well as by black Africans in the Sahara and the Sudan."

According to Dr. Fell the petroglyphs are "script reflected and inverted in the mirror of the water" and would be translated into Modern English as "Plunge in to cleanse and dissolve away impurity and trouble; this is water for ritual ablution before devotions."

As you can see the petroglyphs can inspire the imagination and produce many different explanations as to their origin and their meaning, and with the lack of conclusive, scientific evidence to explain them, many theories are possible.

What's yours?

The petroglyph on the left, found carved in the rocks at the petroglyph pool in Reef Bay was chosen to be the logo for the Caneel Bay Resort.

REEF BAY ESTATE HOUSE

The spur trail to the Reef Bay, or Par Force, Estate House begins on the Lameshur Bay Trail about 100 yards east of the intersection with the Reef Bay Trail. It is a moderate to steep quarter-mile climb to reach the plateau upon which the great house was constructed. See Map 8, page 276.

The Reef Bay Estate House was built in 1832 and reconstructed in 1844. In 1994 it was partially renovated by the National Park Service. The attention to architectural detail and the sturdy construction of this building are noteworthy. As was the custom in plantation days, the cookhouse or kitchen was built as a separate structure. Here the ruins of the cookhouse are located just outside the entrance to the great house.

The National Park Service is fighting a losing battle to keep bats from living in the Estate House. Look for these harmless flying mammals hanging from the ceilings of the building.

The Reef Bay Estate House was the scene of a tragic love story, which can serve to shed some light on the period immediately following the emancipation of the slaves in the Danish West Indies.

On July 3, 1848 governor of the Danish West Indies, Peter Von Scholten issued the following proclamation:

> Maketh known:
> 1. All Unfree in the danish westindia Islands are from to-day emancipated.
> 2. The Estate Negroes retain from three months from date the use of the houses and provisiongrounds, of which they have hitherto been possessed.

Reef Bay Great House

3. Labour is in future to be paid for by agreement, but allowance is to cease.

4. The maintenance of old and infirm, who are not able to work, is until farther determination to be furnished by the late owners.

On July 4 and on July 5, 1848 the proclamation was read on St. John. The St. John Carnival, celebrated on July 4, commemorates this event.

Unfortunately, it seemed that the authorities on St. John had their own interpretation of what "emancipation" meant.

On July 5, 1848 a police placard was posted at Cruz Bay and Coral Bay:

> ...owners and captains of boats and other vessels in St. John...under severe penalty, (are prohibited) to bring persons belonging to the laboring classes away from this island...

On July 10, 1848 another placard was placed at Cruz Bay and Coral Bay. This placard forced the newly "freed" to sign work contracts with their former owners.

A July 26 circular dealt with wages. "Being free the people must support themselves with labor. The wages in money which they receive for their labor should accordingly supply them with nearly the same quantity of food and laboring clothes which they formerly received as allowance. As there were no stores to buy food and clothing it was indicated that actual wages were not necessary, and allowances should be given directly to the laborers."

The "freed" were not free at all. They were not allowed to leave the island, or even the plantation, and they received the same allowance for their labor that they did under slavery.

The post-emancipation era on St. John was characterized by a series of rigid, confusing, and outmoded labor laws. Workers had to sign yearly contracts with their employers, and a maximum wage of two dollars per month was mandated. Many laborers failed to renew their contracts because other more profitable or desirable options existed.

In St. Thomas, for example, labor laws were not enforced, and much higher wages were paid. Laborers were, therefore, tempted to flee St. John in order to work in St. Thomas. One man, who was returned to St. John after being apprehended in St. Thomas, reported that he had been working at the St. Thomas harbor for $1.25 a day. This was a far better wage than the $2.00 a month paid on St. John.

Another escape option for laborers was Tortola. On that British island it was possible to obtain land for farming. Moreover, right on St. John were hundreds of acres of abandoned sugar plantations, where workers could survive on their own by subsistence activities such as provision farming, charcoal production and fishing.

In 1851 a British abolitionist publication, *The Anti-Slavery Reporter* described conditions on St. John:

> The labouring population have nearly the same wages, and are under the same coercive regulation, which, in some late instances, had been exercised with greater severity than the law, severe as it is, could ever have contemplated. Some well-disposed people, helpers in the Moravian Church, had been flogged for slight transgressions of discipline, who had never been flogged as slaves; and we hear of one well-authenticated case, in which a young man, for stealing canes, had been so severely flogged as to die of the lacerations, four days after. The labourers, generally speaking, are abject and crouching, and unwilling to give evidence of the wrongs that come under their notice.

Our story takes place in 1855.

The following is taken from research done by Ruth Hull Low and Rafael (Lito) Valls, in *St. John Backtime*:

In 1855 a young Moravian woman named Elizabeth, age nineteen, lived in the Reef Bay Estate House. She was a servant working for Stapleton Smith, an American. He was a 56-year-old widower and a member of the prestigious Burger Council.

Living with him at the estate house were his two daughters and three younger servants.

Elizabeth had a lover named Henry T. Knevels. He was 26 years old and a member of a prominent Dutch Reform family.

For five years Henry had worked as an overseer at the Par Force estate. During that time he fell in love with Elizabeth. When his employment came to an end at Par Force, he got a new job as overseer at Klein Caneel Bay (Caneel Bay). He wanted Elizabeth to come and live with him there.

Henry Knevels sent the following letter to Judge Carl Hanschell on September 12, 1855:

> I beg leaf to inform you that during the month of warning (when workers could change employers) Elizabeth has been twice to Mr. Smith for her pass to leave Parforce and come to me. This pass has been refused to her, and I have been informed that this refusal made her lament so much that she brought an infant before her time was expired to be delivered. I therefore beg the Humble favor to learn from your Honour if said Woman will be permitted to leave Parforce, having given Legal warning - I must at the same time acquaint you, Honoured Sir that I have lived with Elizabeth for the last five years, during which time I have given her all she has been in

want of. She has also been of infinat service to me during my
miserable living at Parforce, therefore I think it is my duty to
try and do something for her.

Census reports after 1855 make no more mention of Stapleton
Smith or Elizabeth. The 1857 census lists Knevels as single, his
occupation was given as sailor, and he was living in Cruz Bay.
The 1860 census lists him as still single, occupation planter and
still living in Cruz Bay. After 1860 his name is no longer found
on any census lists.

What happened to Elizabeth? This will probably forever remain
a mystery. It has been speculated, though, that she was taken to
America by her employer and was never to see her lover again.

LAMESHUR BAY TRAIL

The Lameshur Bay Trail connects the western part of the beach at Lameshur Bay with the Reef Bay Trail. The 1.8-mile track includes a steep hill that reaches an elevation of 467 feet above sea level. The distance from Lameshur Bay to the Reef Bay sugar factory is 2.6 miles, and from Lameshur Bay to the petroglyphs is 2.1 miles. See Map 8, page 276.

The public road leads right to the trailhead, which is clearly marked by a National Park information sign. (The road to the right goes up the hill and leads to the rangers station and the Bordeaux Mountain Trail.) The ruins of the Lameshur Bay Plantation lie in the immediate vicinity of the trail entrance and can be easily accessed and explored.

There are two spur trails on the route. The first leads to the rubble beach at Europa Bay and the second to the old Reef Bay Estate House.

The Lameshur Bay Trail begins as an easy walk through coastal flatland in a cactus scrub environment. You may see a National Park information sign prohibiting crab hunting. This refers to the land crabs (Cardisoma guanhumi) that live in the holes in the low-lying areas near salt ponds and marshes. They are considered delicacies in the Virgin Islands and Puerto Rico but, as the sign indicates, the land crab is now protected within the National Park boundaries.

Shortly after passing the "no crab hunting" sign, you will come to a large old tamarind tree that has several hollowed out areas in its trunk. Bees often make their hives in these hollows, and you should be able to find an active hive here. In the past beehives were far more abundant than they are today.

Shortly after the trail begins to incline, you will come to the entrance of the Europa Bay Spur Trail on your left. The trail is clearly marked by a National Park information sign. (For details about this trail see the following chapter, Europa Bay Trail.)

Continuing on the main trail, just past the Europa Bay Spur Trail entrance, you will find a stone bench, which was constructed by the American Hiking Society in January of 1986. From here you can look down upon Little Lameshur and Great Lameshur Bays and the Yawzi Point Peninsula that separates the two.

The trail continues up the valley until it crosses over the ridge at a saddle in the mountains. At 467 feet, this is the highest point of the trail, which descends steeply from here on. Loose rocks on the trail can be slippery, so proceed with caution.

A stone wall mottled with lichen can be found just off the trail near the high point. These stones are of volcanic origin and are locally known as blue bitch.

As you descend into the Reef Bay Valley you will be treated to spectacular views of the valley, the outlying bay, the long fringing reef, and the shallow inshore lagoon. (Notice the brighter green and taller trees found alongside the gut in the center of the valley where the water table is close to the surface.)

From this height you will also be able to observe the opening in the reef at the center of the bay. The bluer water at the aperture is deep enough to allow most sailing vessels entry into the protected harbor behind the reef. This feature of Reef Bay supported the development of the sugar plantations in the valley due to the relative ease with which shipments of sugar and rum could be loaded on to ships bound for Europe.

As you approach the lower levels of the valley, you will come to a fork in the trail. The wider, right-hand fork leads up to the Reef Bay Great House. The narrower left hand fork, which passes through a profusion of sansevieria (mother-in-law tongue), leads to the Reef Bay Trail. At the intersection of the Reef Bay Trail, go left to reach the ruins of the Reef Bay Sugar Factory or go right to access the Petroglyph Trail or to continue up to Centerline Road.

land crab

calabash

EUROPA BAY TRAIL

The Europa Bay Trail connects the Lameshur Bay Trail to the rubble beach at Europa Bay. It is 0.3 mile to the beach from the beginning of the spur. See Map 8, page 276.

The trail descends moderately, losing the altitude gained on the Lameshur Bay Trail.

At the bottom of the hill you will come to a salt pond. The shoreline of the pond is easily accessible and you can observe some of the pond's inhabitants, such as birds, ducks, crabs and shrimp.

The trail continues along the flats between the pond and the sea ending at the coral rubble beach at Europa Bay.

Waves generally break over the shallow reef close to shore, but when the sea is flat you can enter the water to snorkel at the north end of the beach. The best snorkeling here (for experienced snorkelers only) is around the point to the south called White Point, but only on extremely calm days.

The beach is cooled by easterly trades and is usually quite deserted, and thus, makes for a great picnic spot, as well as a place to enjoy seclusion and natural beauty.

YAWZI POINT TRAIL

The Yawzi Point Trail begins at the eastern end of the beach at Little Lameshur Bay and ends at the tip of the peninsula at Yawzi Point. This narrow headland divides Great Lameshur from Little Lameshur Bay. The 0.3-mile trail passes through thorny scrub vegetation. See Map 8, page 276.

This peninsula is called Yawzi Point because people infected with yaws, an infectious tropical disease causing destructive skin and bone lesions, were once forced to live, and die, here.

Near the beginning of the trail, about half way up the first hill, you may find an old stone wall that appears to be the foundation of a house.

About 200 yards further down the trail, a short spur to the left (east) leads to a small cove surrounded by large rocks. This beautiful little cove on the shore of Great Lameshur Bay will give you the feeling of being in a secret and hidden place. For experienced snorkelers, this is a good place to access the excellent snorkeling around Yawzi Points. (For details see the snorkeling section chapter, "Yawzi Point", page 255.)

Going on past the spur trail, look for sprays of wild orchids that grow alongside the path.

The Yawzi Point Trail ends at a rocky point where there is a spectacular view of Great Lameshur Bay to the east, and of the southern shore of St. John to the west.

BORDEAUX MOUNTAIN TRAIL

The Bordeaux Mountain Trail runs between Lameshur Bay and the Bordeaux Mountain Road. Centerline Road is 1.7 miles from the point where the trail meets the Bordeaux Road. The Bordeaux Mountain Trail is 1.2 miles long and there is a change in altitude of about 1,000 feet. The grade is, therefore, quite steep. It can be strenuous going uphill and slippery going down. The trick to enjoying this walk is to be sure to pace yourself, watch your footing, and bring sufficient water and sun protection. See Map 8, page 276.

The view from the intersection of Centerline Road and the Bordeaux Mountain Road, near the Chateau Bordeaux Restaurant was chosen as one of the ten best views in the Caribbean by *Caribbean Travel and Life Magazine*, in its April 1996, tenth anniversary issue.

The environment around the trail changes with the elevation. The higher sections of the mountain receive more rainfall and experience cooler average temperatures than lower areas. Thus, if you begin your hike at the bottom of the trail you will first pass through cactus scrubland, as you ascend you will move into dry forest, and at the highest elevations you will enter a shady and cool moist forest.

At the bottom of the trail are the ruins of the old Lameshur Bay Plantation. Exploring these ruins, you will find the bay rum distillery, the sugar factory and the boiling bench. You will also find a residence, a well, and an animal trough that dates back to the more recent subsistence farming days on St. John.

In the early part of the twentieth century, this estate was dedicated mainly to the production of bay rum oil. Bay rum trees were cultivated on the upper regions of Bordeaux Mountain, where you will see (and smell) many of these smooth-barked aromatic trees. This trail was once used to transport the bay rum leaves harvested on Bordeaux Mountain, via donkeys, to the bay rum distillery located at the beach at Lameshur Bay.

If you begin your walk from the beach, the first part of the trail will be the steep four-wheel-drive road leading up to the National Park ranger station. A picturesque old stone wall covered with bromeliads lines the dirt track. Just about a quarter mile from the beach, the trail forks with the road to the ranger station turning off to the right and the Bordeaux Mountain foot trail continuing up the mountain. The trail is marked by a National Park information sign that reads: "Bordeaux Mountain 1.0 mile".

The trail is rocky and steep as it climbs along the western edge of the Great Lameshur Bay Valley. Occasionally swales made of rocks cross the path. These rudimentary conduits serve to divert rainwater across the trail instead of allowing it to flow directly down the trail. Thus, the swales serve to prevent rutting and erosion, which would normally result when the natural vegetation has been disturbed.

Look for a sign with information about the Bordeaux Trail rehabilitation project. About 100 yards past this sign you will find a seat, suitable for one person, made of dry stacked stone with a flat top. Take advantage of this rustic resting-place, which was put together by members of the trail crew. You should find more of these seats along the way, though some have been damaged by hurricanes.

When the trail turns toward the right, you will come to a large tree growing by the side of the path, next to which are some flat rocks to sit on. Growing out of the tree is a strangler fig. There is a beautiful view from here, which looks down into Great Lameshur Bay and out at Yawzi Point between Great and Little Lameshur Bays. To the southeast is an excellent view of Ram Head Point.

Just before the trail switches back to the left for the first time, there is a narrow spur trail to your right. This leads to a small, shady plateau and the remains of a charcoal pit. Look for a tamarind and a genip tree and a small stand of teyer palms. The ground cover is love leaf.

As you ascend from here you will notice more changes in the environment. You will pass an area of the spiny pinguin, or false pineapple, which produces a citrus-like fruit. You will begin to see genip trees as well as other dry forest trees such as the reddish, shiny-barked turpentine, and the attractive black caper. As you progress up the trail you will see guavaberry and bay rum trees, vegetation common to the moist forest.

You may find another stone seat in this vicinity, also made by the trail volunteers. At this elevation you can see over the saddle in the mountains to the Sir Francis Drake Channel and British Virgin Islands. After a few more switchbacks through the shady forest, you will reach the end of the trail, which emerges at the Bordeaux Mountain Road.

Across the road are the ruins of the Bordeaux Plantation. The sugar factory was built between 1790 and 1820 during St. John's best sugar production years. It was a T-shaped factory representative of that period. In this case, however, a piece of the "T" is missing. It was destroyed by the road crew during the construction of the Bordeaux Mountain Road.

The boiling bench is still visible, as well as two rum stills and two cooling cisterns. Parts of the canning room also still exist. On the other side of the road are the remains of a slave village. The estate house for the plantation is up the hill on a knoll. There are three well-preserved graves near the estate house.

The plantation was founded by Thomas Bordeaux in the 1720s. He was a Frenchman who came to the Danish West Indies, now known as the United States Virgin Islands, along with other Frenchmen as a result of the revocation of the Edict of Mann, which allowed the French government to persecute the Protestants known as Huguenots. Thomas Bordeaux, who was a prominent citizen in St. Thomas, came to the Danish West Indies directly from France. Although he was the owner of the property, he probably never lived on the plantation.

Bordeaux Plantation was later owned by Jean Malville, a Moravian of French ancestry. Malville was born in the Danish West Indies and became the first native-born governor of the islands. During the time of his ownership the plantation was called Malvilleberg.

SALT POND AND DRUNK BAY TRAIL

The Salt Pond and Drunk Bay Trail begins at the eastern end of Salt Pond beach and heads inland (left) towards the salt pond. It is an easy quarter-mile walk with no hills. The trail skirts the western edge of the salt pond and continues on to the rocky windswept beach at Drunk Bay. See Map 7, page 275.

Salt pond

The bottom of the salt pond is made up of a layer of red algae giving the salt pond a reddish-brown color. The distinctive smell of the pond comes from another layer of older red algae, which is found just below an intermediate layer of sand.

Look for the delicate blooms of the beautiful wild orchids along the trail and watch for donkeys, deer and birds especially in the early morning.

Because of its location on this arid and windswept part of the island, Salt Pond is the most likely place to encounter crystallized salt. Saltwater enters the pond from the sea by seepage at high tides and by waves breaking over the surface during storms. Salt Pond is one of the only places on St. John that is below sea level. This condition prevents significant amounts of pond water from flowing back out to sea. Constant, intense sunlight and ever-present tradewinds encourage an exceptionally high rate of evaporation. When rain is scarce, the water becomes extremely salty. Water can only hold a certain amount of salt in solution and when the salinity of the pond reaches that point, the salt dissolved in the water crystallizes.

As the water level continues to drop, and more and more water is evaporated, a layer of salt is left along the edges of the pond. The longer the dry period, the higher the temperature, and the stronger the winds, the more this salt layer will extend towards the center of the pond and the thicker the layer becomes.

You can collect salt during these times by scooping up the salt with your hands, if it is still wet and soft. If the salt layer is dry and hard, use a knife or other sharp tool. (If you've forgotten to bring a container, just walk over to nearby Drunk Bay where there is a great deal of flotsam, and you'll probably find something you can use.) After the salt is collected, drain off as much water as possible and put it in the sun to dry further. You may be left with fine powdery salt, which you can enjoy on your food immediately. If the dried crystals are large, you will first need to grind them up or pound them out.

The salt obtained from salt ponds is particularly tasty and healthy. It contains all the minerals that are present in the sea, which include all those essential to the human body. So during the next dry spell, take the short and easy Drunk Bay Trail from Salt Pond Bay over to the salt pond and bring home a sample of this delicious and nutritious natural salt.

Enjoy the experience!

Drunk Bay

The trail continues to the rocky windswept beach at Drunk Bay. The easterly trades bring ashore an abundance of flotsam, which makes for great beach combing. In these modern pirate days of drug smuggling, bales of cocaine and marijuana have reportedly been washed up along this shore.

RAM HEAD TRAIL

The National Park website describes the Ram Head Trail as follows: *Ram Head Trail (1.0 mile, 1 hour) - Trail starts at the south end of Salt Pond Bay Beach. This rocky, exposed trail leads to a unique blue cobble beach and then switchbacks up the hillside to its crest 200 feet above the Caribbean Sea. Magnificent windswept scenery. DANGER: Watch your footing near the cliff edge.*

See Map 7, page 275.

This walk can be particularly sunny and hot, so bring water and sun protection. For this reason, the best time to take this hike is early in the morning when it is still cool, possibly before sunrise.

Visiting Ram Head at sunrise, sunset and full moon can be an impressive experience. Those choosing to undertake this adventure, however, should exercise extreme caution. The steep, narrow and slippery path, which can be tricky enough during the day, is even more perilous during periods of low light. Bring a flashlight and walk slowly and carefully.

The trail to Ram Head Point begins at the eastern end the beach at Salt Pond Bay. Begin by walking along the small rocks and coral rubble along the eastern shore of the bay.

The West Indian top shell, locally called whelks, can be found adhered to the rocks near the water line. They are an island delicacy and are often prepared during carnival time.

After about 100 yards, a defined trail begins and leads up through the cactus forest. It ascends to an elevation of about 100 feet and then descends to sea level. There are great views along

Lignum Vitae

Lignum vitae means "long life" in Latin and another name for this tree is Tree of Life.

Before the European colonization, which led to the deforestation of St. John, there were many stands of Lignum vitae on the island. They helped to produce a jungle-like canopy over large portions of the island, providing shade for tropical undergrowth.

On St. John, most large native trees were cut down to prepare for sugarcane cultivation or were harvested for their valuable wood. Once plentiful on the island, the Lignum vitae is now relatively rare. Notwithstanding, beautiful mature lignum vitae trees can be seen near the Post Office, on the corner near the Texaco station, by the sugar mill at Caneel Bay and along the Ram Head Trail. Many new Lignum vitae trees have been planted by people such as Hermon Smith, Andy Rutnik and especially by the late Ivan Jadan.

The wood of the Lignum vitae is exceptionally hard and dense. It resists rot caused by insects and moisture. Remains of Lignum vitae wood used as posts for dwellings by Taino Indians were discovered in Tutu, St. Thomas. These posts dated by carbon dating were found to be over 800 years old. In colonial days this hard, strong, and long-lasting wood was an invaluable construction material.

Lignum vitae wood was once used in the past to make ball bearings because its extremely high resin content makes it self-lubricating. Another place that Lignum vitae were used was in United States courtrooms, where the judge's gavel was traditionally made from this fine wood.

The bark of the Lignum vitae, especially on the lower part of the trunk, is smooth in texture and purple and green in color. The tree tends to branch out early and may have multiple trunks, which form a large and relatively low canopy. The leaves are bright green. When the tree blooms, usually in the late spring or early summer, it produces small blue flowers, which later develop into bright orange fruits.

the whole length of the Ram Head Trail, however a particularly fine vantage point can be found at the top of this hill.

Lignum vitae

There are four mature Lignum vitae trees growing right along-side the trail near the top of the first hill. This is one of the few places on the island where you will still find mature Lignum vitae trees.

Blue Cobblestone Beach

The path descends to a blue cobblestone beach. This beach may be a destination in itself providing uncrowded swimming conditions and access to excellent snorkeling just north of the beach. For details about the beach and snorkeling see the chapter entitled "Blue Cobblestone Beach", page 249.

On to Ram Head Point

The trail to Ram Head begins again at the south end of the beach. Walk along the coast until you see the path marked by a National Park information sign.

This section of trail gains elevation through a series of switch-backs and proceeds up the hill to the saddle area of the peninsula. The predominant plant species here is the barrel or Turk's head cactus. Attractive black caper trees, identified by their dark bark and narrow leaves, are also abundant in this area. You will often see wild goats grazing along the rocky hillside. These goats have degraded the environment by eating much of the vegetation, resulting in the erosion of the topsoil in times of rain. Only the hardiest species of plants yet survive.

At the top of this hill you come to the saddle or low point between two hills. A fault line cuts across the narrow peninsula here. The views are dramatic. You can look down the cliffs on the eastern side and see waves crashing onto the small cobblestone beach between the cliffs. The view to the west is tranquil and serene, in stark contrast to the windy and rugged eastern exposure.

barrel cactus

The air

The eastern coast of Ram Head Point is totally exposed to the tradewinds. If you were sailing east from here, your next land-fall would be Africa. The air you will be breathing on this beach is arguably the cleanest, freshest and most invigorating air in the world.

The trail switches back several times through a cactus environment and leads to the tip of Ram Head Point.

Geologically, the rock that makes up this headland is the oldest rock found on St. John. Evidence supporting this theory was gained when geologists, using diamond tipped drills, bored into the rock at Ram Head. They drilled down over one half a mile before breaking through the last of the rock. The new substance brought up by the drill was examined and shown to be the same material that makes up the ocean floor, indicating that no other rock was there before it.

History

It has been speculated that this remote and inhospitable region provided a hideout for runaway slaves, called maroons, who lived here just before the slave rebellion in 1733.

This was a time of severe drought on St. John. Food could not be easily grown and was in scarce supply. The biggest problem the maroons faced was finding fresh water. The underground springs had dried up along with the freshwater pools of the major guts.

On Ram Head, however, the maroons could provide themselves with food and water. Water could be found stored in the cactus that proliferated on the peninsula and the waters around the point provided excellent fishing. Whelks could be picked along the rocky portions of the coast, and conch could be harvested on the grassy seabed of Salt Pond Bay.

For these reasons Ram Head is thought to have been a stronghold for the Akwamu tribesman who rebelled against slavery in 1733. When the tides of battle turned against the rebels, a group of warriors committed suicide here rather than face capture.

St. John Backtime, by Ruth Low and Lito Valls, contains an account of this mass suicide in the chapter, "Only Enough to Shoot Themselves". At a court deposition an eight year old boy named January gave this account of the suicide:

> He declared that the Company's Kanta, Suhm's Autria, Runnel's Coffie, Horn's Tjamba, Krøyer's Acra and another, Soetman's Sepuse, and three females, the Company's Bragatu and two others named Acubo and Bomboe, belonging to he knew not whom, committed suicide at Ram's Head. They had six guns to kill themselves with; the last to kill himself broke up five of the guns and shot himself with the sixth; Kanta the last one, first stabbed him (January) with a knife to kill him, but he fled and hid in the bush;...G.H. Nissen, Town Clerk.

(January is a St. John family name, and members of this family may be descendants of this young man.)

The peak

"Stand at Ram Head Point and feel yourself merge with the wind. Absorb the sounds and smells of the sea. Delight at the beautiful sight of unspoiled nature around you, as far as you can see in every direction. Go in the morning, at noon or at night. Go for sunrise or sunset on the full moon and watch one rise and the other sets opposite it, both huge on the same horizon. Go during the new moon and try all night to count the stars. Ram Head Point is an experience you will keep forever."

Ram Head Point description, courtesy of Constance Wallace.

section two

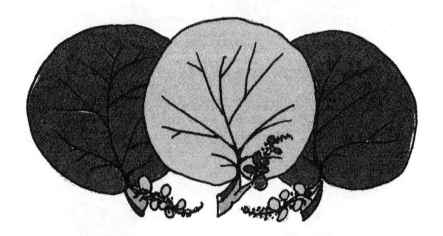

OTHER TRAILS,
HIKES AND
SCRAMBLES

LIND POINT ROCK SCRAMBLE

The Lind Point Rock Scramble takes you from downtown Cruz Bay to Salomon Bay Beach by way of the rocky coast. The walk is a little less than one mile.

The natural pathways found on St. John, an island of thick forest and tangled undergrowth, generally follow the ridges of mountains, natural drainage guts, or shorelines. Most of the trails made by Amerindian and early European settlers, and even the modern roads found on St. John today, follow these natural paths.

The shoreline between Cruz Bay and Salomon Bay is typical of many coastal sections of St. John. Those interested in experiencing this environment will have to make their way through a section of mangroves and then climb up and down the rocks that line the shore. This adventure should only be attempted by two or more athletic individuals who have experience in rock scrambling. It is extremely important that you proceed with the utmost caution and are aware and attentive at all times.

A good place to begin this walk is at the old seaplane ramp in Cruz Bay. See Map 1, page 269.

There is no defined trail. Begin by finding your way through the tangle of mangroves that extend for about 50 yards along the shore. This may be the most difficult portion of the walk. Remember that wet rocks may be slippery.

Once through the mangroves you will be negotiating rocky shoreline interspersed with sections of beach.

Heading west along the coast of Cruz Bay Harbor, you can observe the barges, ferries, sailing yachts and small motor boats entering and exiting the bay. At the mouth of the harbor the rocks get taller, and the scramble gets more dramatic. Right after the coastline begins to turn north, you will come to a cobblestone beach at Lind Point. An old, now unused, underwater telephone cable comes ashore here.

The coastline between Lind Point and Salomon Bay is undeveloped and pristine. Take some time to observe the coastal marine life that has developed with only minimal impact from the activities of human beings.

East of Lind Point you will come to a small coral rubble beach. There are three types of beaches on St. John, white coral sand, cobblestone and coral rubble. It is interesting to note that all three can be found along this short stretch of coastline. For more information on the nature of St. John beaches see page 214.

Immediately after the tiny coral rubble beach, you will come to a larger cobblestone beach. Just past the vegetation line are large pieces of galvanized roofing that once were on National Park housing units up the hill on Lind Point. Imagine the force of the wind that was able to carry this heavy metal roofing such a long distance. (A hurricane in 1916 blew the roof off of the Methodist Church in Great Harbour, Jost Van Dyke. It was later found at Cinnamon Bay on St. John, more than five miles away.)

Continue the scramble until you get to the sand beach at Salomon Bay. For those so inclined, this is an excellent opportunity to reward yourself with a refreshing swim.

You can return to Cruz Bay the way you came or via the Lind Point Trail. For trail details see page 13.

BROWN BAY SHORELINE WALK

The beautiful and secluded beach at Brown Bay can be reached by following the St. John shoreline between Waterlemon Beach and Brown Bay. See Maps 4 and 5, pages 272 and 273. This entire hike is characterized by spectacular views and refreshing tropical breezes. It is definitely off the beaten track, however, and demands athletic ability and knowledge of rock scrambling. Don't attempt this (or any) hike alone and be careful!

Begin by taking the three-quarter mile Leinster Bay Trail from the Annaberg Sugar Mill parking lot to the beach at Waterlemon Bay. The shoreline walk between Waterlemon Bay and Brown Bay Beach is about a mile and a half long. Allow at least four hours for a leisurely and careful roundtrip journey from Annaberg to Brown Bay and back.

Once you arrive at the beach at Waterlemon Bay, follow the shoreline north. There is a rudimentary trail that will take you a short distance along the coast, but when that ends you will be on your own. At the saddle between the hills, just before you get to the tip of the headland called Leinster Point, you may find a donkey trail that will lead you across the peninsula, or you may just find it easier to walk and scramble around the point.

On the eastern side of Leinster Point you will come to a coral and cobblestone beach fringed by beach maho trees. The ground cover is the salty, but edible, sea purslane. A shallow fringing reef lies just off the beach.

Scramble over the black rocks at the end of the beach or take a donkey trail through the bush and go around them. On the other side of the rocks is a coral rubble beach. There is no reef on the western corner of the beach and you can get into the water and take a cooling swim if you so desire. At the center of the beach are several water mampoo, or loblolly trees that can provide a welcome shady area where you can rest and enjoy your surroundings.

The view from this beach is impressive. To the west, you can see the top of Mary Point and the headland called Leinster Point that you just crossed. These two headlands define the well-protected Leinster Bay. Looking more to the north you will see the British islands, Great Thatch and Little Thatch. Between them, further to the north, is Jost Van Dyke. Tortola is the large island just to the east of Great and Little Thatch. The tall mountain that you see on Tortola is called Sage Mountain, which at 1740 feet is the highest point in the Virgin Islands.

At the end of the beach you will come to some high rocks. The scramble over these rocks is facilitated by the presence of conveniently located hand and foot holds. On the other side of these rocks is a coral rubble beach backdropped by a steep bluff about 40 feet high.

At the end of this beach, a short scramble leads to another stretch of coral rubble beach bordered by a high steep hillside and fringed by century plants and seagrape trees. At the end of this beach is a stretch of rocky shoreline which leads around Threadneedle Point. This is a colorful, impressive and secluded area. To the east you can see the British Virgin Islands that border the beautiful Sir Francis Drake Channel all the way to the Baths at Virgin Gorda and looking west you can see as far as St. Thomas and Hans Lollik.

After rounding Threadneedle Point there will be one more long stretch of coral rubble beach. From there to the beach at Brown Bay is a section of rocky coast, which goes past the Brown Bay plantation ruins.

You can return to civilization the way you came or via the Brown Bay Trail. For further information, see the chapters on the Leinster Bay, Johnny Horn and Brown Bay Trails and Brown Bay, in the beach and snorkeling section.

REEF BAY COASTAL WALK

The Reef Bay Coastal Walk provides an alternative route to the historic Reef Bay Sugar Mill, the petroglyphs and the Reef Bay Estate House. By taking short trails, walking along the beach and scrambling around small headlands, one can cover the entire perimeter of Reef Bay. The distance between the Reef Bay sugar mill ruins and Parrot Bay on the western end of Reef Bay is about 1.2 miles.

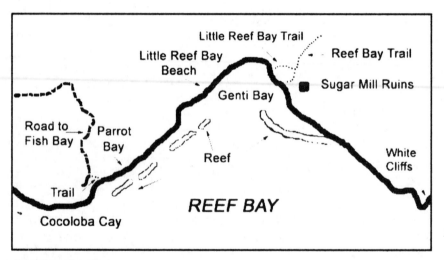

About the bay

Reef Bay refers to the large bay on the south side of St. John between Cocoloba Cay on the west and the White Cliffs on the east. Within the larger bay are three beaches one of which is an inner bay. On the west is a beach called Reef Bay or Parrot Bay. The next beach to the east is Little Reef Bay, named after the plantation whose ruins lie amidst the vegetation behind the beach. The third and easternmost beach makes up most of the shoreline of Genti Bay, which is an inner bay of Reef Bay. Genti Bay is the location of the Reef Bay sugar factory ruins, which lie at the end of the Reef Bay Trail.

A long line of reef extends parallel to the shoreline of Reef Bay. The reef protects the beaches and coastline from the force of the ocean swells. An extensive shallow lagoon lies between the shore and the reef.

The Name

Parrot Bay was named after Rif Paret, an overseer on the Friis plantation established in 1727 on the western portion of Reef Bay.

The larger Reef Bay, that encompasses Parrot, Little Reef and Genti Bays, may also have been named after Rif Paret. Old maps of Reef Bay show various spellings of the word Reef including Rif, Riif, Riff, Rift and possibly Riss.

Eminent St. John historian, David Knight, feels that the name Reef Bay is really a corruption of "Rift Bay" pointing out "that the original name for this quarter was Rift Bay and not Reef Bay."

There also exists the possibility that Reef Bay was named after the long barrier reef that is the most significant characteristic of the bay.

Directions

Only Parrot Bay at the western end of Reef Bay can be accessed by road. From the Texaco Station in Cruz Bay, take the South Shore Road (Route 104) east to the Fish Bay Road. Go 1.7 miles to the intersection of Marina Drive and Reef Bay Road. Bear left onto Reef Bay Road and go up the hill. Turn left after the concrete strip of road ends, about 0.2 mile from the intersection. Go 0.2 mile further and park on the right side of the road across from the house with the wooden shingle roof.

The path to the beach starts at the utility pole. The top of the trail is steep. You will find a length of knotted rope secured to various trees that you can grab onto for support as you descend this steepest section of the trail. Be careful on the rest of the path, as it too can be tricky and slippery at times, especially after a rain. At the bottom of the hill, the trail levels off and leads to the beach at Parrot Bay.

Walk east along the white sandy beach. It is a delightful walk as there is generally a brisk and cooling ocean breeze. You will also be treated to the sight and sound of the waves breaking over the outer reef as well as to an excellent view of the unspoiled south coast of St. John from Reef Bay to Ram Head Point and into the inner valleys of Reef Bay. This is one of the few large areas in the Virgin Islands that has not been developed and remains in a pristine and natural state.

Much of the ground cover at the beginning of the line of first vegetation is the edible sea purslane. Further inland are seagrape and beach maho trees interspersed with areas of mangroves.

About 30 yards before the end of the beach there is a small coconut grove just inland. It's easy to get to and if you're in luck there will be lots of coconuts to eat - hard ripe ones on the ground and the even more delicious jelly nuts up in the tree.

At the eastern end of the beach you will come to some colorful red and white rocks around the point going left. It's an easy scramble over these rocks to the beach at Little Reef Bay.

The shallow lagoon gets much wider here. This is a habitat for baby sharks, tarpon, bonefish and barracuda. The baby sharks, mostly black tips, are quite a sight to behold. They are between one and two feet long and, because the water is so shallow, their dorsal fins stick out of the water, just like in the movies. Don't worry about them biting you, they are very shy and timid and swim away as soon as they see you.

As you walk down the beach at Little Reef Bay you will have an extensive view of the south coast. The only human-made structure in sight will be the chimney of the Reef Bay Sugar Mill abandoned almost a century ago.

A narrow strip of soft white sand, fringed by maho trees and mangroves, lies between the lagoon and the forested interior. Behind this vegetation is an area of low-lying flat land that began to be cultivated in 1726, eight years after the Danish West India and Guinea Company colonized St. John.

History

Of the twelve plantations in the Reef Bay watershed, Little Reef Bay was the only one that never engaged in sugar cultivation and was instead dedicated to cotton, provision crops, and the raising of cattle and other livestock. Little Reef Bay historically provided much of the food for the neighboring sugar producing estates of Reef Bay.

The first owner of the land was Philip Adam Dietrichs, a Lutheran priest in St. Thomas. Because pastors received a minimal salary in those times, the governor of the colony presented the estate to Dietrichs in order to help him make ends meet.

The task of clearing the land, planting the crops and building the needed structures was performed by a small number of slaves who worked from sunup to sundown on that arid and windswept parcel of land in order to provide a supplementary income for the underpaid man of God. Because Dietrichs lived in St. Thomas where he continued to minister to his parishioners, an overseer was hired to wield the whip and be responsible for the success of this marginally profitable enterprise.

Dietrichs eventually left St. Thomas and returned to Denmark. The estate was sold to Jannes Runnels and stayed in the Runnels family for about the next 100 years.

In 1841 Catherine Michel, a free woman of mixed race, inherited the Little Reef Bay plantation along with 26 head of cattle, 40 sheep, 8 horses and 27 enslaved human beings. It was a hard life for all concerned, Catherine Michel, her six children, and the slaves. When emancipation was declared in 1848, there were only two acres of land under cultivation to support the Michel family and the slaves, who were predominantly women and children.

Even after emancipation in the Danish West Indies, the former slaves were bound to their estates by labor contracts, which they were forced to sign. The "workers" on the Little Reef Bay Estate were reluctant to continue laboring on that unproductive and poor piece of land. Catherine Michel was ill, as were her children, and by 1870 all had died, apparently of the dread disease leprosy.

Little Reef Bay was then sold to Henry Marsh who owned the neighboring Par Force plantation where the sugar works were. In 1926 it was sold to A. A. Richardson, the island administrator, who had 30 acres of land under cultivation and a herd of 25 cattle. Richardson sold milk, mangos, coconuts, bananas and limes that were produced on the estate.

In 1956 Little Reef Bay became the property of the Virgin Islands National Park.

(Information about the history of the Little Reef Bay Estate comes from *A Brief History of the Little Reef Bay Estate*, by David

Knight and *Historic Land Use in the Reef Bay Fish Bay and Hawksnest Watersheds, St. John U.S. Virgin Islands* by George F. Tyson.)

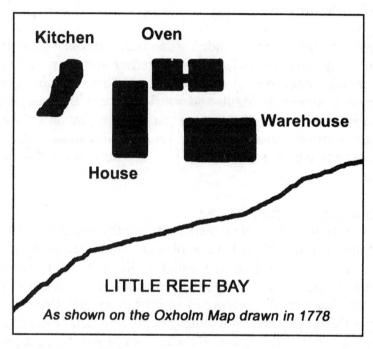

As shown on the Oxholm Map drawn in 1778

Finding the ruins

The ruins of the Little Reef Bay Plantation can be found just about ten yards inshore of a patch of mother-in-law tongue or snake plant (Sansevieria), that were once cultivated as an ornamental, but got out of hand. They consist of long, pointed, variegated, dark-green leaves that rise from the ground to a height of about three feet and grow close together. The patch extends right to the beach line. Another clue is a tall date palm that you should be able to see further inland than the ruins.

If you're not keen on plant identification, here's another way to find them: As you walk down the beach towards the east, there are two places where vegetation extends into the water. At these points you will either have to get your feet wet, climb through the tangle of limbs, or find a passage through the bush inland. The remains of the Little Reef Bay plantation lie behind the second of these detours.

The ruins consist of a four-sided stone wall that once supported a house made out of sticks woven together and then plastered with mortar made out of lime and mud. This traditional construction is known as "daub and wattle." Just to the east of the house is a taller wall that was a part of the plantation warehouse. Also in the vicinity are the remains of a stone oven and the kitchen, which traditionally was separate from the main house.

Turn of the century house

Just to the east of the warehouse ruins are the remains of an old stone house covered with pink plaster. There are ornamental plants and fruit trees near the building. In back of this house is a stately date palm. Mother-in-law tongue, hibiscus and bougainvillea are all growing in profusion around these ruins. Most of these plants were obviously cultivated as landscaping by the inhabitants of the house. Near the house are the remains of an old cattle corral, a remnant of the fairly recent cattle-farming operation in the valley. The estate house and warehouse were built in the late eighteenth century; this house was built near the turn of the twentieth century.

History of the house

When the Little Reef Bay Estate was sold to Henry Marsh, a one-acre parcel was split off and given to the one loyal servant, named Margreth, who stayed with Catherine Michel and her family throughout the days of deprivation and the horrors of leprosy. The house had remained in fair condition, roof and all, until Hurricane Marilyn struck in 1995. This property is called an inholding because it is still privately owned and is not part of the National Park. The lack of access to this and other inholdings in the park is currently a much-discussed political issue.

Swimming beach
The best place for swimming in Reef Bay is at the eastern end of the beach, near the rocks along the eastern shore (to your left if you're looking out to sea). The beach is soft white sand, and the entrance to the water is in sand and grass. The water is deeper and the bottom is sandier and more comfortable than the beaches at either Parrot Bay or Genti Bay. Another plus is the almost guaranteed privacy afforded by the remote location.

The Little Reef Bay Trail
At the eastern end of the beach, the trail to the Reef Bay Sugar Mill begins about thirty yards from the first large rocks. At the beginning of this trail is an old stone cistern and animal watering trough surrounded by hibiscus and bougainvillea.

The Little Reef Bay Trail connects the beach at Little Reef Bay with the bottom of the Reef Bay Trail near the sugar mill ruins. The well-maintained path is a little over a quarter-mile long and passes over the rocky point separating Genti Bay from Little Reef Bay.

The trail goes up a hill and then down again reaching an elevation of about 75 feet. The environment is one of disturbed, second growth cactus scrub.

History of the trail
Not long ago the Little Reef Bay Trail did not even have a name. The account of how this trail became a clear readily passable pathway with an actual name goes like this:

The highly popular guided Reef Bay Trail hike, organized by the National Park and conducted by knowledgeable rangers, includes boat transportation from the end of the trail at Genti Bay back to Cruz Bay. This eliminates the necessity of the highly unpopular uphill walk back to Centerline Road.

Before Hurricane Marilyn in 1995, there was a dock at Genti Bay. Hikers were brought by dinghy from the dock to a larger boat that would then make the voyage to Cruz Bay. After Hurricane Marilyn destroyed the dock, the tour operators attempted to board their passengers onto the dinghy from the shallow water near the shore. Because there are often waves breaking near the beach, the task of loading the dinghies with people unaccustomed to small boats proved to be difficult and dangerous.

As an alternative to building another dock, it was decided that Little Reef Bay, which is generally calm at the eastern end, would be a safe place to put the hikers aboard the dinghy. (Years ago, the only dock in the valley was on the eastern end of Little Reef Bay because this was the only place in all of Reef Bay to have protection from the wind, waves and swells while still having deep water access.)

The trail from Little Reef Bay to Genti Bay was then cleaned up by park employed workers and has been given a high priority for maintenance ever since.

COCOLOBA CAY COASTAL WALK

The three-quarter mile Cocoloba Cay Coastal Walk takes you around Oyen Point between Fish Bay and Reef Bay on the south coast of St. John. The walk begins at the Fish Bay dock and leads to the rocks overlooking Reef Bay. There are no hills and no defined trails. See Map 9, page 277.

From the Texaco Station in Cruz Bay, take the South Shore Road (Route 104) east to the Fish Bay Road. Go 1.7 miles to the intersection of Marina Drive and Reef Bay Road. Bear right on Marina Drive. After you pass Guavaberry Farms Nursery, the road gets a bit steep and rugged. From here to the dock a four wheel drive vehicle and off-road driving experience is highly recommended. Park near the dock at the end of the road.

This little known area in the mangroves is used by local residents with small boats and by fisherman who fish off the dock.

From the dock at Fish Bay you can often see small fish and baby sharks that spend their early lives in the shallow waters near the mangroves. This is one of the largest mangrove basin forests on St. John. Many fish come here to breed. The fresh water entering from the three major guts of Fish Bay keep the salinity of the water low and the nutrient level high.

South of the dock (to your left looking out at the bay) there is a trail that leads through the mangroves. The trail ends at some large black rocks at the water's edge. There is an opening between the rocks that leads to the shoreline.

You will have arrived at a small shallow lagoon protected by off-shore reef. Ocean swells often break over the reef. Surfers and boogie boarders can ride these waves in the summertime when the southerly winds are strong and the south swells wrap around the point and roll into Fish Bay.

Along the edge of the small lagoon, the shoreline consists of rocks, coral rubble and patches of sand. A view of the bay opens up as the coastline curves toward the east. About fifty yards after Cocoloba Cay comes into sight, you will arrive at a long sandy area referred to as Cocoloba Beach.

Cocoloba Cay

This remote and secluded sand and coral rubble beach is probably the most private of all St. John beaches. It is an excellent location for relaxation, contemplation and reflection.

Cocoloba is not good for swimming. The water is shallow with many sea urchins among the rocks. There is generally a strong current and breaking surf. On calm days though, experienced snorkelers can enter the water fairly easily, and there is good snorkeling along the reef and around Cocoloba Cay.

The beach ends at an area of large black rocks. Continuing along the rugged shoreline you will come to a point where you will be treated to views of the pristine south shore of St. John. Looking inland you will see a steep rocky hillside. Incredibly, there are century plants, cactus and sea grapes growing in this inhospitable environment where there is hardly any soil.

The colorful red and white rocks in this area are unique to the south shore of the island. The red color is the result of a high iron content. This section of coast is exposed to the easterly tradewinds and is usually windy. There may be some interesting flotsam washed up along the shore.

Just before you get to the tip of Oyen Point that divides Fish Bay from Reef Bay, you will come to a small and secluded sandy section of shoreline surrounded by large rocks. To continue you will need to scramble over these jagged red rocks.

When you get to the end of the point, you can climb higher up on the rocks for a bird's eye view. This is a secluded and dramatic setting where you will be surrounded by the sounds of wind and waves.

Looking to the east, you will see the western beach at Reef Bay, called Parrot Bay. Further to the east are the Reef Bay Valley, Genti Bay, the White Cliffs, and the practically uninhabited south shore, stretching all the way to Ram Head. To the south are St. Croix and the open Caribbean. To the west is Cocoloba Cay. Looking down into the clear water you can see the rocks and reef below the surface. This is one of those increasingly rare places, where you can enjoy a beautiful panoramic view that remains completely undisturbed by development.

From here it is possible to continue climbing the rocks along the shoreline to Reef Bay, but it is difficult and can be dangerous. A better option would be to turn around and go back to the dock.

FISH BAY AND BATTERY GUTS

The terrain of St. John is mostly mountainous. Between the mountains are valleys. When it rains, water seeks its lowest level, flows and seeps down the hillsides of the valleys, and makes its way down toward the sea. In the Virgin Islands these rain-collecting temporary valley streams are called guts.

When it rains hard, water rushes down the guts taking with it soil and sediment that have collected during dry periods. The bottoms of the guts are left as bare rocks. Along the edges of the guts, the plant life grows profusely due to the abundance of water available to them. These gut environments are usually tropical and jungle-like.

Some of the most accessible and beautiful guts are in the Fish Bay area. Most often hiked are the Fish Bay and Battery Guts, which come together at an elevation of about 200 feet in the Fish Bay Valley.

These are difficult and challenging hikes and should only be undertaken by those in good physical condition and who possess knowledge of rock scrambling techniques. It is extremely important to exercise the utmost caution. The rocks may be slippery and the ways out of the gut and back to civilization are limited. Do not attempt this (or any) hike alone!

The Fish Bay and Battery Guts, along with the Living Gut in Reef Bay and the Guinea Gut, are the only south side guts that have some degree of permanent water. Pools and waterfalls along the gut provide homes for several species of freshwater fish, crabs and crayfish.

The gut environment is dynamic. It will change considerably depending upon the amount of rainfall and the time of year. The hike along these natural pathways will, therefore, vary in difficulty, and you will have to be creative at times to find the best ways around obstacles such as waterfalls, pools, fallen trees, thorny vines and unfriendly plants.

The Fish Bay Gut can best be accessed from the Fish Bay Road on either side of the bridge that crosses the gut. See Maps 10 and 11, pages 278 and 279.

In this low-lying area the gut can be crowded with thick vegetation, but getting through is not as difficult as it looks. Be prepared to get wet especially in the early morning when there is a lot of dew on the grass or after a night of showers. As the elevation begins to increase, there is less vegetation in the gut, and the going is easier.

The tall trees along the sides of the gut filter the sunlight and create an exciting tropical atmosphere. Watch for orchids growing in the nooks and crannies of trees and rocks. You will find bright green moss, lush tropical ferns, and an assortment of flowering trees and other plants.

Freshwater pools
The freshwater pools contain fish whose eggs can lie dormant for years at a time when the pools dry up. They will hatch when there is sufficient rainfall to support life in the pool. Also look for freshwater crabs, which scurry for shelter when they see you approach, and crayfish that look like little Maine lobsters. Colorful dragonflies often hover above the pools. Here the forest is alive with the buzzing of bees and the songs of birds attracted to the water in the pools.

After about a quarter mile you will come to the intersection of the Fish Bay and Battery Guts.

Battery Gut
The Battery Gut is the western (left) fork and continues up alongside the Gifft Hill Valley, where it begins in the vicinity of Neptune Richard's Laundromat. On the way it passes the Pine Peace School where there is an exit trail.

The waterfall
About 0.1 mile from the gut intersection is a seventy-foot high waterfall. There are fresh water pools on the top and bottom of the cliff. The base of this waterfall is a wonderful place to stop and relax for a while before the return trip down the gut.

Experienced rock climbers, however, can climb this steep rock face, which offers a variety of hand and foot holds. Above the waterfall, the gut becomes more overgrown. There is access from the Battery Gut to Gifft Hill Road next to the Pine Peace School. This narrow trail will be on your left as you ascend the gut.

During the slave rebellion of 1733 the Free Negro Corps led by Mingo Tamarin pursued a party of rebellious slaves down the gut from Beverhoudtsberg Plantation where a battle, which was then called a batterie, was fought at the bottom of the high waterfall. The Battery Gut was named after this battle.

Fish Bay Gut
At the intersection of the two guts the eastern (right) branch is the Fish Bay Gut, which leads to Centerline Road running for a time alongside the old L'Esperance Road. There are several opportunities along the way to access the L'Esperance Road before climbing through the increasingly thick underbrush as you approach the upper levels of the valley and Centerline Road. The rarely traveled L'Esperance Road will provide much easier

access to Centerline Road and civilization.

The Fish Bay Gut has several fresh water pools as well as a beautiful waterfall that descends much more gradually than the Battery Gut waterfall; be extremely careful climbing the waterfall because the rocks can be very slippery.

MAHO BAY GOAT TRAIL

The Maho Bay Goat Trail connects the Maho Bay Campground with the North Shore Road (Route 20). It begins near the northern portion of the beach at (Big) Maho Bay where the road turns sharply to the right and inland. See Map 3, page 271.

This scenic trail serves as a shortcut between the North Shore Road at Big Maho Bay Beach and the Campground at Little Maho Bay.

It is a ten to fifteen minute uphill walk from Big Maho Bay to the campground. On the upper portions of the trail, you will be treated to excellent views of Maho Bay Beach and the north shore of St. John. The two tamarind trees at the top of the trail provide a shady place to sit and rest on the exposed roots between the two trees.

The trail ends below the commissary at Maho Bay Campground. From here the beach at Little Maho can be reached by a series of wooden stairs down to the bay.

Ethel McCully

Ethel McCully, author and colorful St. John personality, made her home at Little Maho Bay from 1953 until her death in 1980. In those days the North Shore Road was only a rough dirt track. It ended at the goat trail, which was the only access to her property.

The story of how Ethel McCully discovered Little Maho is a St. John legend.

Ethel McCully had been working as a secretary in New York. On her vacations she would often come to the Caribbean where she had dreams of someday buying her own house. On one particular winter vacation in 1947 Ethel McCully had gone to the island of St. Thomas in the United States Virgin Islands. From there she booked passage on a Tortola sloop bound for Tortola in the British Virgin Islands.

On the tack that would take the sloop out through Fungi Passage and into the Narrows, the boat passed close by Little Maho Bay. Ethel McCully was enthralled by the sight of the small, perfect beach backdropped by emerald green mountain valleys. She asked the skipper to allow her to go ashore to explore. He replied that it was not permitted because he had already cleared out of United States territory.

Ethel McCully announced that if she could not be taken ashore, she would swim. The crew helped her over the side, and she did just that.

She later bought the property and built a house on the bluff above the bay. She did this with the help of six donkeys and two laborers. Ethel wrote a book about the experience that was to be titled; *I Did It With Donkeys*. Her publisher said "no" to this idea, and the book was published in 1954 with the title, *Grandma Raised the Roof*. The roof to her guesthouse, which she called Island Fancy, was actually raised in 1953. Before her literary success with *Grandma Raised the Roof*, Ethel McCully was a mystery writer and an ambulance driver during World War One.

Ethel McCully fight against condemnation

In 1962 St. Johnians discovered at the eleventh hour that a bill giving the Secretary of the Interior the power to increase the National Park's landholdings through condemnation was up for final vote in the United States House of Representatives. Ethel McCully and other St. Johnians, including the late Senator

Theovald Moorehead (better known as Mooie) went to Washington in an effort to persuade Congress to defeat the proposed amendment. Mooie talked to congressmen and senators and placed an ad in the Washington Post. Mrs. McCully spoke at a meeting of the United States House of Representatives and expressed her ideas about the condemnation amendment.

The following is quoted from an article published in the *New York Times* on September 9, 1962 by J. Anthony Lukas entitled *Grandmother Fights Congress*.

> A 66-year old grandmother is planning to "raise a little hell" on Capitol Hill this week.
>
> One official had a preview yesterday of the way Mrs. Ethel Waldbridge McCully planned to defend her home in the Virgin Islands from condemnation under a bill before Congress.
>
> The official warned her that a Congressman she planned to approach was "a very difficult man."
>
> "Well I'm a very difficult woman," Mrs. McCully told the startled official. So that will make two of us."
>
> Mrs. McCully, tiny and fragile looking, built her tropical hideaway on the lush, green shore of St. John Island, one of the three main islands in the United States territory in the Caribbean.
>
> A successful mystery-story writer, she described her construction task in a book called *Grandma Raised the Roof*, published in 1954.
>
> But she said yesterday:
>
> "You can change that title now. You can call it 'Grandma Raises Hell'. Yes, you can say I'm going to raise a little Hell."

Ask some of the older St. Johnians if they remember Ethel McCully and you may be treated to some entertaining stories.

Ethel McCully died in 1980 at the age of ninety-four. Island Fancy now belongs to the National Park.

Erva Thorp

In the late 1950s Erva Thorp, the former Erva Boulon and her husband Bill built and ran a guesthouse at Little Maho Bay that was called Lille Maho, the old name for Little Maho Bay. Andy Rutnik, Commissioner of Licensing and Consumer Affairs in the administration of Governor Turnbull, and his wife, Janet Cook Rutnik, now an internationally recognized artist, used to be the caretakers of Lille Maho for Mrs. Thorp.

AMERICA HILL TRAIL

The America Hill Trail begins along the Cinnamon Bay Trail about 50 yards past the first gut crossing and leads to the ruins of the Estate House at America Hill. These ruins can be seen from Maho Bay, on the hill to the west. (See Map 2, page 270.)

Do not climb on or go too close to the ruins as they are in an unstable and dangerous condition.

The trail runs uphill and switches back five times before you reach the mountain plateau, which is the location of the great house ruins. Much of the trail is lined by the sweet lime bush, also known as limeberry bush, a plant whose thorns can be somewhat unfriendly to hikers if left to grow out over the trail. The limeberry produces a fragrant flower and an edible fruit, used in making jams and jellies.

An old sugar boiling pot will be visible on the left just before you arrive at the end of the trail and the remains of the crumbling estate house.

The America Hill Estate House is an excellent example of late nineteenth century Virgin Island architecture. Much attention was obviously given to an aesthetically pleasing design as well as to functionality, the limitations of the building site, and the availability of materials and labor.

In the early 1900s it served as a guesthouse where travelers could rent rooms. One of the last tenants was rumored to be Rafael Leónides Trujillo, former dictator of the Dominican Republic.

Some older St. Johnians say that the estate house was also used as a headquarters for rumrunners during the prohibition days.

As was the custom in those days the cookhouse or kitchen was built as a separate structure. The remains of the cookhouse for the America Hill great house are to the right of the main building. The date 1934 is inscribed on the cooking bench. To the left of the estate house ruins are the remnants of a cistern and a well.

Although the estate house is now completely surrounded by dense vegetation, the view must have been spectacular when the house was occupied. Looking through the bush you can see Maho Bay, Francis Bay and Mary's Point on St. John and White Bay on Jost Van Dyke. Also visible are Tortola's north coast, Great Thatch, and part of Sir Francis Drake Channel.

DITLEFF POINT

The Ditleff Point Trail begins at the Fish Bay Road and follows the ridgeline over the headland to the rocky cliffs at the tip of Ditleff Point. The distance is about three-quarters of a mile and the grades are moderate. The maximum elevation gained will be approximately 100 feet. See Map 10, page 278.

Directions

Starting from Cruz Bay, take the South Shore Road (Route 104) east to Fish Bay Road. Proceed 0.6 miles along the Fish Bay Road until you come to a concrete road on your right called Klein Bay Road. Don't turn! Continue on the Fish Bay Road, which descends and curves towards the left. Turn right just before the next utility pole. This will be a dirt road that extends about forty feet and ends with a mound of dirt. Leave your car here and continue on foot. The trail begins behind the dirt mound and through an open iron gate with stone pillars.

Although the road is privately owned and goes through undeveloped private property, it has become the traditional access for Virgin Islanders to get to the beach at Ditleff Point.

From Fish Bay Road to Ditleff Beach (north end)

The Ditleff Point Trail follows the old road through a cactus scrub environment. The predominant vegetation is the scrubby wild tamarind, catch-and-keep, century plants, acacia, and pipe organ cactus.

At the top of the first small hill you will have your first view of Ditleff Beach, which will be on the western side of the point.

As the trail descends, you will pass through an area of the coarse

158 OTHER TRAILS, SCRAMBLES, AND PLACES OF INTEREST

and fragrant maran bush. This was used in the past as a pot scrubber and deodorizer. Most of the bigger trees in this area are mampoo trees. Look for air plants and wild orchids growing in the trees and rocks.

At the bottom of the hill you will find the intersection of two trails. The one to the right, or west, leads to the northern end of Ditleff Beach.

Ditleff Beach (West)

Ditleff Beach is a small protected bay with a stretch of shoreline consisting of sand and broken up pieces of coral. Hurricane Marilyn brought back the sand that Hurricane Hugo took away, and a new layer of sand extends past the vegetation line. One can now relax in soft sand and still enjoy the shade produced by the maho and seagrape trees that line the beach.

The Ditleff Peninsula protects the bay from the easterly tradewinds, and the water near the beach is generally calm. The bottom of the bay is seagrass and sand. Because the beach faces west there is strong afternoon sun.

This is one of the few sand beaches on the island that is still relatively private and secluded and is a wonderful place to spend the day relaxing, exploring, picnicking, swimming and snorkeling. (See chapter on the snorkeling Ditleff Point, page 257.)

A coastal walk

From the beach it is possible to walk along the shore towards a dramatic rocky point. An extensive fringing reef protects the coast and beach from the action of southeasterly swells coming in from the Caribbean. This shallow reef also creates a series of small tide pools. You can often observe small fish and crustaceans within this miniature environment.

Further south along the coast there is a narrow shallow passage between the peninsula are some large offshore rock formations where small fish and marine creatures can be observed. There is a beautiful and dramatic view through this passage.

A photograph of this view appears on the cover of this book.

Northeastern coast

Returning to the first intersection on the main trail, the left or eastern trail leads to an overlook with a view of the eastern coast of Ditleff Point, Fish Bay, Cocoloba Cay, and the pristine southern coast of St. John all the way to the Ram Head peninsula. From this overlook there is a steep and slippery path to the shoreline below, where there are a series of small sand and coral rubble beaches. The first few beaches are behind the back reef. The water is shallow and unsuitable for swimming. However, by walking and rock scrambling north (left, looking out at the water) toward the inner harbor, you will reach an area of deeper water where you can enjoy a nice private swim. The difficult access to this part of the Fish Bay coast insures your privacy.

Be extremely careful scrambling the rugged and rocky path from the main trail to the water's edge.

The saddle area

The main Ditleff Point Trail continues south along the ridge. You will go up a small hill and then down again. At the next low point there is another trail intersection. The trail to the east goes to the rocky beach on the Fish Bay side of the point. The trail to the west goes to the southern end of Ditleff Beach. The ruins of an old house, partly hidden by bush, can be found near the beach, just south of this path.

At the trail intersection on the ridge, it is possible to stand in one spot, and by turning to the east or to the west, have an entirely different perspective of the environment. Facing the strong tradewinds to the east, the sea is dark blue and deep, often with whitecaps and breaking waves. To the west, the bay is protected, its turquoise waters calm and shallow.

The rocky beach at the end of the left, or eastern, spur is exposed to the tradewinds and can have breaking surf. The foliage is low, pushed down by the pressure of the almost constant winds. You may notice that much of this low-lying vegetation is seagrape, which has adapted to this rugged environment by remaining low and shrub like. Sea grape trees in calmer areas, like those on the calm western side of the peninsula, can grow into rather tall trees.

This beach offers fantastic views, excellent beachcombing, and cool, clean, refreshing breezes.

The exposed coastline, shallow reef, and breaking waves, however, make the beach unsuitable for swimming.

From the saddle to the point
The main path continues up again. Nothing grows tall here. The wind keeps the plant life low. Maran bush and thorny acacia line the trail.

This path is rarely traveled, and you will surely pass through many spider webs made by the harmless golden orb spider.

Golden Orb Spider (Nephila clavipes)

The golden orb spider or golden silk spider is one of the many spiders in the orb weaver family. The orb weaver makes webs sometimes reaching from 15-20 feet. The golden orb is the only spider known to make its webs strong enough to be used for various kinds of bags and fishnets. Although this spider does not sting, the females are known to eat their mates after sex.

Erik Chapman with queen conch

Gibney Beach

students from the Guy Benjamin School studying underwater ecology

view of Cruz Bay from the Lind Point Battery Overlook

brick, coral and native stone wall found at Brown Bay

sugar works and bay rum factory at Cinnamon Bay

calabash

broom making at the Annaberg sugar mill cultural fair

basket making at the Annaberg cultural fair

Coral Bay, East End and the Sir Francis Drake Passage seen from Bordeaux Mountain

inside the windmill at Cathrineberg

yacht at anchor

hawksbill turtle

frangipani caterpillar

Christ of the Caribbean on Peace Hill before Hurricane Marilyn in 1995

night blooming cerius

grouper

America Hill estate house

Jumbie Bay

Reef Bay sugar mill

angelfish

At the top of the hill, the old bulldozed road ends in a turn-around. The path, however, continues south into the bush where the native frangipani with its beautiful and extremely fragrant flowers grows in abundance.

When the trail emerges from the forest, you will arrive at a sun-drenched and windswept clearing. The predominant plant found here is the barrel cactus, which bears edible pink fruit.

On the east are sheer cliffs. There are two places where you can stand at the edge of the precipice and experience this remarkable and dramatic view. Strong breezes blow in from the sea and the sky is often filled with seabirds riding the rising air currents.

As you approach the point, the trail begins to deteriorate. You can still make your way over rocks and cactus and through patches of guinea grass to the tip of the peninsula. This point of land is now called Ditleff Point. In the past it was known as Rendezvous Point, and pronounced "REN dey who".

The View
The panorama from the top of the point is spectacular. To the east you can see the entire southern coast of St. John, including Ram Head, Salt Pond, Kiddle and Grootpan Bays, the Lameshur Bays, the White Cliffs, Reef Bay, Fish Bay and Cocoloba Beach. Looking south and west you can see St. Croix, Frenchcap Cay, Buck Island off the coast of St. Thomas, Dog Island and Dog Rocks, Little St. James, Great St. James, St. Thomas, Bovocoap Point and Rendezvous Bay in its entirety with its inner bays of Hart, Monte, Klein and Ditleff.

St. John Riddle...

WHAT
HAS
THREE
EYES

BUT
CANNOT
SEE?

answer
a coconut

CATHARINEBERG

The Catharineberg ruins are now the property of the National Park and may be visited by the public. Going east (towards Coral Bay) on Centerline Road, just past mile marker "3", turn left onto John Head Road. The Catharineberg windmill will be on your right about 50 yards from the intersection. See Map 2, page 270.

The windmill has been restored, and it is in excellent condition. An old stone warehouse with arched passageways can be found beneath the windmill. Across the road are the remains of the horsemill, the rum still, and the sugar factory. The windmill is an excellent place to take children, who will enjoy exploring the passageways and tunnels. A good time to visit the windmill is at night, especially during full moon; remember to bring a flashlight.

The horsemill, across the road from the windmill has been converted to a cistern and now serves as a fresh water pond containing attractive aquatic plants.

The remains of the sugar factory and rum still are near the intersection of Centerline Road and John Head Road.

Look for the tiny "sensitive plants" near the road in front of the windmill. They will react to your touch by closing their leaves.

History
The Catharineberg plantation was founded in 1718 just after the Danish colonization of St. John. It was 150 acres and was owned by Judith Ann Delicat. In the same vicinity as Catharineberg, two 75-acre plantations named Jochumsdahl A and Jochumsdahl B

were started in the same year. They were also owned by the Delicat family. These plantations were consolidated into one 300-acre property called Jochumsdahl/Catharineberg, Catharineberg or Herman Farm.

By 1721 Catharineberg was harvesting sugarcane and the following year a sugar factory was completed.

In 1797 at the peak of the sugar boom 107 people lived at Catharineberg. 150 acres were devoted to sugar and 150 acres to other crops. There was no unimproved land on the plantation.

Sugar declined as an important crop during the nineteenth century and Catharineberg discontinued production in 1896. By then most of the estate was devoted to stock raising and by 1915 Catharineberg had ceased operations.

During the 1940s an American named Cory Bishop operated a small farm on the old estate.

FREDRIKSDAL AREA

The Fredriksdal area, south of Mary Point, was once the most populated section of St. John. There were plantations at Maho Bay, Mary Point, Fredriksdal, Annaberg, Leinster Bay and Windberg. The historical ruins and places of interest can be accessed via the North Shore Road (Route 20), south of Leinster Bay Road. This is an excellent area for a leisurely stroll. The terrain is relatively flat, and the surrounding forest is shady and lush. The historical sites are close to the road and easy to get to. The more intrepid can make their way further into the bush to explore the area to a greater degree. See map below and Map 3, page 271.

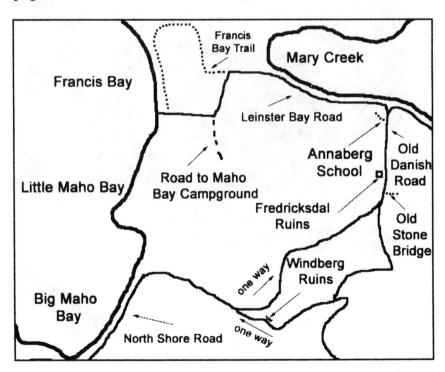

Old Danish Road

The National Park has cleared a section of an old Danish road, so that you can see what the island roads looked like back in colonial times. The cleared section of old road is located right near the intersection of the North Shore Road and Leinster Bay Road, just across from the Annaberg School.

Fredriksdal

Fredriksdal was named for Frederick Von Moth who lived on St. Thomas. He purchased it from Reimert Sødtmann, magistrate of St. John in the early 1730s. (Sødtmann and his stepdaughter were among the first victims of the slave rebellion in 1733.) Von Moth was commander of the civil guard on St. Thomas and later became governor of St. Croix.

The grand entrance and stairway of the Fredriksdal ruins are the remains of the estate house, which served as living quarters for the owners of Annaberg Plantation and are visible from the road. There are extensive ruins extending back into the bush. They include the remains of an oven, a well, a horsemill and other old structures and walls.

The area is covered with thorny sweet lime as well as catch and keep, so wear appropriate clothes to explore.

Old Stone Bridge

Across the road from the Fredriksdal ruins is a seldom-used trail that was once part of the Old Danish Road. It leads to a fairly well preserved stone bridge that is almost hidden in the thick bush. Note the depth and the width of the gut and the height of the bridge. To necessitate the building of such an elaborate bridge, there must have been a regularly flowing stream here in the past. The fact that the streambed is now almost always dry indicates that the amount of rainfall on St. John has decreased substantially over the years.

Windberg

Just east of Big Maho Bay, the North Shore Road splits into two one way roads. The Windberg ruins are located on the side of the road that heads back toward Big Maho Bay and Cruz Bay.

Slaves on the Windberg Plantation, as well as on plantations all over the island, did anything in their power to resist the conditions to which they were subjected. These acts of resistance included such tactics as shipboard mutiny aboard slave ships, overt rebellion such as the violent and almost successful slave rebellion of 1733, suicide, self-mutilation, abortion and marooning or running away from the plantation. They resisted as well by pressing for the enforcement of already established laws, which had been passed by Danish liberals to improve the conditions of slavery, and by conducting labor actions, such as strikes, work stoppages and sick-outs.

In 1831 the slaves at Windberg staged such an action. Forty slaves reported to be ill and checked into the plantation sick house. The overseer on the plantation reacted by forcing the slaves to work. One woman died, and the police conducted an investigation. The overseer was fired, and a new overseer was brought in. The new overseer, reluctant to use extreme force, was faced with the difficult task of restoring the plantation regime. He was neither feared nor respected and was unsuccessful in compelling the slaves to go back to work. Windberg remained in a state of disorder until the landfoged (island administrator) intervened on the overseer's and owner's behalf.

RUSTENBERG

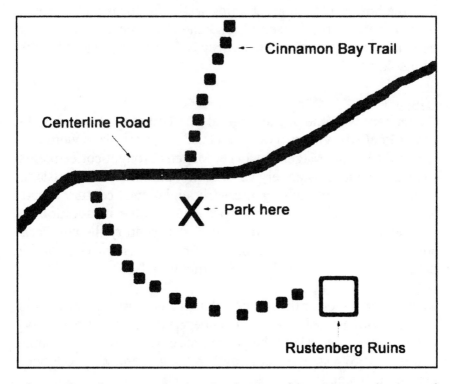

The trail to the Rustenberg ruins begins about 200 yards west of the head of the Cinnamon Bay trailhead on Centerline Road. Park your vehicle off the road across from the Cinnamon Bay trailhead and walk up Centerline Road the short distance to the Rustenberg Trail, which leads south and will be on your left.

The trail to these exciting and extensive ruins is a little over a quarter mile and leads through a shady forest environment. The plentiful bay rum trees in the area provide a refreshing fragrance as you walk along the level and narrow path. Once you arrive at the ruins there will be spur trails leading to various parts of the old plantation and sugar works.

Look for the remains of the horsemill with the storage room built into the horsemill's stone retaining wall. The sugar boiling room is right next to the horsemill, and the old coppers and boiling benches are still in evidence. Nearby is the cooling cistern for the rum still.

History

Rustenberg was one of the original 12 plantations located within the Reef Bay Valley. Two parcels of 150 acres each were distributed to Jacob Magens in 1718. Magens brought coffee plants to St. John, and Rustenberg was the first plantation on the island to grow that crop. During the early eighteenth century Estate Rustenberg produced cotton, cocoa and coffee in addition to sugarcane. Towards the latter part of that century the emphasis shifted to sugar production, and by 1767 the vast majority of the plantation acreage was devoted to that crop.

During the nineteenth century the profitability of sugar was declining on St. John and Rustenberg, like many other sugar plantations on the island, began to phase out production. A hurricane in 1867 was the last straw, and sugarcane was no longer grown at Rustenberg.

During the first part of the twentieth century the area around Rustenberg experienced a brief economic comeback by growing and harvesting bay rum.

FORT FREDERIKSVAERN

Fort Frederiksvaern is located at Fortsberg, a peninsula that juts out into Coral Bay separating Coral Harbor from Hurricane Hole. It is on private property owned by the Samuels family. Ask Fred Samuels at Fred's Bar and Restaurant in Cruz Bay for permission to visit the fort.

Directions
Take Centerline Road (Route 10) east about a half mile past the Moravian Church in Coral Bay. Turn right on the dirt road near the Flamingo Club. The road follows the coast of Coral Harbor before ascending a steep hill and coming to a fork. The left fork goes up to the fort and the right fork goes down to the water battery. There are magnificent views along both of these roads.

History
Frederiksvaern, constructed at the top of the 400-foot high hill at Fortsberg, was first completed in the early 1720s. At that time only twelve soldiers stationed there. They were armed with a few cannons and a small supply of rifles and ammunition.

In 1780 the fort was intentionally destroyed but archeological evidence indicates that it may have been at least partially reconstructed since then. A round stone wall surrounded by an outer circle of pinguin were the first lines of defense. Within the stone walls of the fort were the commandant's headquarters, a powder magazine, housing for five soldiers, four gun emplacements, a cookhouse and a mess hall. Three eight-pound cannons covered the approach from the land, and a sixteen-pound cannon faced the sea. Six more cannons were located at the water battery below the fortification. The cannons at the water battery still exist.

On November 23, 1733 a group of slaves carrying concealed cane knives killed six of the seven soldiers stationed at the fort and fired a cannon to announce the beginning of the historic St. John Slave Rebellion.

> A number of Negroes from the warlike Amina nation took control of the fort while fulfilling their accustomed job of supplying the place with firewood. They struck down the small contingent of soldiers there with knives, which they had hidden in their bundles of firewood. After they gave their fellow conspirators the agreed-upon signal for the uprising - several cannon shots - the rebellion spread to all the parts of the island...
>
> C.G.A. Oldendorp, *History of the Evangelical Brethren on the Caribbean Islands of St. Thomas, St. Croix and St. John.*

Fort Frederiksvaern is listed in the National Registry of Historic Sites.

Pinguin

Pinguin is a member of the bromeliad family. They were probably brought to the Virgin Islands by the native Amerindians.

The individual plants grow close together and have numerous barbed spines that stick out every which way. This makes pinguin extremely difficult to pass through. Early European settlers took advantage of this characteristic and used the pinguin as a living fence.

The pinguin is also called false pineapple because of its great resemblance to the true pineapple. It produces a large attractive flower that is followed by a cluster of edible yellow fruits, which have a pleasant and mildly tart taste.

ST. JOHN SLAVE REBELLION

The slave trade

The Danish colonization of St. John was undertaken in 1718 for the purpose of establishing plantations where tropical products such as sugar, cotton, indigo and other crops could be cultivated. The most profitable of these crops was sugar.

Sugar production in the West Indies was an extremely lucrative affair. The sudden introduction of sugar to Europe created a great demand for this exotic new product. With this high demand and preciously small supply, the price of sugar was high, and the profit potential was enormous. Many of those involved in this new industry were able to accumulate great wealth and power. It has been said that the only present day business comparable to the sugar trade of the colonial days is drug trafficking.

European colonial powers battled fiercely over control of the new colonies. Pirates and privateers infested the seas in an orgy of murder and plunder. Worst of all was the development of slavery as an institution in the Americas. Slave labor was employed for the exploitation, settlement, and development of the new territories.

When the Spanish first invaded and colonized the New World, they attempted to use the indigenous population as a slave labor force. Disease brought by the Europeans, warfare, cruel treatment, and overwork all but wiped out this race within a short time.

When the Danes occupied St. Thomas in 1672 there were no indigenous inhabitants living there, nor were there any on St.

John in 1718. Therefore, the possibility of obtaining slave labor from this source was not available to the Danes.

The Danish government and the government-supported and subsidized Danish West India Company tried to encourage young Danes to emigrate to St. Thomas to labor on the plantations. Very few responded. Prisoners were then brought over to work as indentured servants with the stipulation that they would receive their freedom after six years, though few would survive that long. Apart from this, indentured servitude was exactly the same as slavery. They lived, ate and worked with the slaves and were subject to the same arbitrary punishments. Their social position was of the lowest order and they were looked down upon by both Africans and Europeans. The prisoners viewed emigration to the colonies as a death sentence. Their desperation and discontent resulted in mutinies and resistance. In response, the Danes began to place more emphasis on the importation of slave labor from Africa.

The first African slaves were brought to Hispaniola in 1502, and slavery was not completely abolished until the early twentieth century. During this roughly four hundred year span, it has been estimated that as many as 12 million Africans were unwillingly transported to the Americas.

A form of slavery existed within Africa prior to the advent of European colonialism. Tribalism has been a major influence in African political history, and warfare between rival tribes was a common occurrence. Many of the Africans who were sold into slavery were prisoners captured in these tribal wars.

The institution of slavery that developed in the colonization of the Americas was, first and foremost, a business. It was characterized by the profit motive, greed, and lacked morality, compassion and human decency. The Europeans' need for cheap labor created the demand. The existence of slaves acquired through the persistent warring of African nations provided the supply. Thus, a market and trade for human beings was established.

The captives were brought to the European forts or slave factories. The factors, or buyers, at the fort would buy the slaves using a barter system. The slaves were then chained and stored in warehouses called barrcoons until the slave ships arrived.

The Danes maintained such a fort at Accra on the Guinea Coast called Christianborg. The Danish West India and Guinea Company sent company ships bearing items such as rum, firearms, gunpowder, clothing and other goods, which were bartered for ivory, gold and slaves to the tribal leaders controlling the trade.

The voyage to the New World was known as the Middle Passage. Captives were confined into such small areas that it was impossible to stand or even sit. Inside the ship's holds, it was dark, dank and stuffy. There was no proper ventilation or sanitary facilities. The ship's officers and crew were made up of the prisoners, misfits and outcasts of Europe. Women were subjected to rapes and indignities. Disease, desperation and suicide claimed many lives before the ships even reached their final destinations in America or the West Indies.

Upon arrival the slaves were sold at public auction and then marched to the plantations for a period of "seasoning". One third of these new arrivals from Africa, called bussals, died during the seasoning period.

Early Danish settlement
The Danish West India and Guinea Company was chartered in 1671 and given the right to govern and exploit Denmark's first

colony in the New World - St. Thomas. The company was granted a royal charter to St. John from the King of Denmark in 1717 and St. John was under company rule until King Frederick of Denmark terminated this agreement in 1755.

Twenty five settlers (eleven Dutch, nine Danes and five Frenchmen), sixteen enslaved Africans, and five Danish soldiers, under the command of Axel Dahl, sailed to St. John in the company of the governor of St. Thomas, Erik Bredal. They landed in Coral Bay on the east end of the island.

Seventeenth century Denmark had marginal resources and a relatively small population of approximately one half million people. Moreover, the Danes were reluctant to emigrate to the new colonies and Denmark lacked a sufficient population to effectively occupy their new territories. To compensate for this, foreigners were invited into the population of the colonies.

The largest and most influential of these foreigners to settle in St. Thomas, and later to settle on St. John, were Dutch. By 1721, of the 39 planters on St. John there were 25 Dutchmen and only 9 Danes. The Dutch, more than any other national group, influenced the culture of the Danish colonies, which prior to the acquisition of St. Croix in 1733, consisted only of St. Thomas and St. John. The most important language was Dutch and Dutch Creole became the "lingua franca" of the Danish islands.

By 1733 more than 1,000 slaves labored on 109 plantations on St. John. Twenty-one of these plantations were in the business of planting and processing sugar. The rest grew cotton and other crops. By the end of the century, however, the vast majority of the plantations were dedicated to sugar production, and there were more than 2,500 slaves on the island. On average, one slave was used for the cultivation of each acre of land.

African background of the rebellion

As early as the beginning of the seventeenth century, Accra on the Guinea Coast had become a center of economic power. The Accra tribe acted as the middleman in the exchange of slaves, gold and ivory from the interior for manufactured goods such as firearms, powder, lead, rum and cloth from the Europeans who operated out of fortifications on the coast.

The Danes entered the slave trade in 1657 by attacking the Swedes who were already established on the West Coast of Africa. By the beginning of the eighteenth century, the Danish West India and Guinea Company had consolidated their slave operation to the vicinity of Accra and traded with the Accra tribe.

All travel and transportation from the interior to the coast occurred along narrow forest paths. The Accras used another tribe, the Akwamu, whom the Danes called the Amina, to control the passage of merchants and merchandise along these trails. This was done so that all goods from the interior would have to pass through an Accra-dominated area north of the region's capital, Great Accra. Thus, direct access to the Europeans was denied to the traders from the interior, and merchants were forced to have the Accras as middlemen. For this unwanted service, the Accras demanded a percentage of the profits of this lucrative trade.

As time went on, the Akwamu, who had been paying tribute to the Accras, became more powerful. They directly controlled the paths leading from the inland centers to the European commanded forts on the coast. Realizing their power, the Akwamu demanded a tribute in gold from the Accras in order to permit traders to pass through Akwamu territory. In the 1670s the Akwamus allied themselves with the Accras' neighboring tribes, the Agaves to the east and the Agonas to the west. These alliances put further pressure on the Accras.

The Akwamus were excellent warriors. They developed an improved military strategy specific to the conditions imposed by the heavily forested environment. They also emphasized the use of missile weaponry, such as bows and arrows and flintlock rifles, which they obtained from the Europeans.

In 1677 the Akwamus attacked and conquered the Accras. Through a series of violent and bloody military campaigns, the Akwamus became the dominant tribe in the district of Accra, along the lower Gold Coast and the Upper Slave Coast.

Thousands were killed, and many prisoners were taken. The Accras, former allies and trading partners of the Danes, fled to the fort at Christianborg seeking protection. The commanders of the fort chose to remain neutral and did nothing to stop the slaughter and capture of the Accras.

The Akwamus were heavy-handed in dealing with the tribes they had conquered. They forcibly conscripted troops from the conquered tribes, demanded tributes and payments, levied excessive taxes, and resorted to the instigation of disputes and other forms of trickery and unfair tactics to justify the enslavement of peoples from the conquered tribes.

For example, I. Akwamu Wilks in *The Rise of the Akwamu Empire, 1650-1710,* wrote:

> In every town (the Akwamu) took some wives, three or four according to the size of the town, and left them there to stay. Then every year they would travel from place to place, and make these wives eat fetish (That is, swear to tell the truth on pain of death from divine power) so that they would confess what men had had contact with them. These disclosures were made willingly, since the women would get part of the fines,

and the gallants might be sold as slaves unless their friends ransomed them.

The Akwamu abuse of power eventually led to resistance and rebellion from the tyrannized peoples. When the Akwamu king died in 1725, a conflict arose over who would take power. This weakened the Akwamus, and the conquered peoples of the area attacked the Akwamu nation. By 1730 the Akwamu were defeated, their capital city destroyed, and their reigning king beheaded.

Once again the oppressed became the oppressors and thousands of Akwamu men and women were sold into slavery. Many of these Akwamus were sold to the Danes at the fort in Christianborg in the early part of the 1730s. They were then placed on ships bound for the slave market in St. Thomas. Many were sold to plantations on St. John.

From the company's records:

> Haabet Galley, Danish registry, Captain A.H. Hammer, came to St. Thomas, February 1731, to sell 21 men 29 women, 5 boys, total of 55 out of Guinea; Cost to company wholesale 70 rigsdalers, cost to planter 120 rigsdalers.

From the company's records:

> Laarburg Galley, Danish registry, Captain Lorenzo Jaeger (replaced by Captain Hammer) May 1733. It carried 443 captives out of Guinea of whom 242 survived (124 men, 64 women, 26, boys, 28 girls); 199 died of dysentery and two were sold to the Portuguese. The ship made an overall profit of 69.5% from the survivors; cost to company; 70 rigsdalers, cost to planters; 120-150 rigsdalers. (From MAPes MONDe Collection)

In 1733 at the time of the slave rebellion there were hundreds of Akwamu men and women among the slave population of St. John. Of the approximately 150 Africans who were involved in the rebellion, all were Akwamus. Africans of other ethnic backgrounds, some of whom had been sold into slavery by the Akwamus, did not support the rebellion. Some even joined the Europeans against the Akwamus.

The Akwamus on St. John did not see themselves as slaves, but rather as slave owners. Many were nobles, wealthy merchants or powerful warriors who were accustomed to large commands.

Information on the African background came from Sandra F. Greene's research appearing in *The Danish West Indian Slave Trade*, by George F. Tyson and Arnold R. Highfield.

Causes of the rebellion

Weakness of the central government and the military
As previously mentioned, Denmark, a comparatively weak nation, began their colonization of the New World later than the other European colonial powers. St. Thomas and St. John were rocky, mountainous, and lacked a significant amount of rainfall. The Danes were able to colonize and settle these islands mainly because none of the other Europeans showed much interest in acquiring this territory.

Without a sufficient number of their own citizens to inhabit their new colonies, Denmark invited peoples of other nations to settle them. Thus, foreigners exerted a strong influence on government decisions.

The plantations were only marginally profitable, and the Danish West India Company lacked the motivation and the resources to provide a strong army for the defense of the islands. They relied instead on a citizen's militia. On St. John this situation bordered on the absurd. Aside from the ineffective civil guard, the number of soldiers stationed on St. John at the time of the slave rebellion numbered six. Moreover, morale was low and the incidence of disease, alcoholism and mortality were high.

Absentee ownership of plantations

Many of St. John's plantations were owned by men and women from St. Thomas who also had estates on that island. The St. Thomians usually hired overseers called Mesterknegte to manage their holdings on St. John. These overseers were not always honest and often failed to act in the best interests of the planters. (Out of sight, out of mind.) The overseers certainly did not give the interests of the slaves much attention.

Low ratio of European to Africans on St. John

Partly because many of the plantation owners and their families lived in St. Thomas, and partly due to the nature of the plantation system itself, the ratio of European planters to African slaves on St. John became extremely low. The lack of a town or any alternative industries also contributed to this low ratio.

Drought, starvation and marooning

On St. John slaves were required to provide the labor necessary to grow the food they ate. They did this on their own plots of land, which were cultivated in their spare time. Because there was no supervision by the owners or overseers, slaves could use the time spent tending these grounds to talk freely among themselves and to make plans.

In 1725 and 1726 and again in 1733, St. John experienced prolonged droughts, and the provision grounds could not yield sufficient food; the slaves faced starvation.

In 1733 much of the land on St. John was not yet cleared and there were still large areas of thick bush and forest. The opportunities provided by this environment, combined with the skills the slaves developed from tending their provision grounds, made it possible for them to run away from the plantation. They were able to disappear into the bush and provide for themselves by tending small gardens, gathering and fishing. The fierce and warlike Akwamu (or Aminas as they were called by the Danes) also demanded the support of slaves still on the plantations.

By 1733 starvation, overwork, and harsh treatment had caused a significant number of slaves from the Amina tribe to maroon.

Slave Code of 1733
The drought of 1733 ended with a severe hurricane in July. This was followed by a plague of insects. Both plantation crops and provision grounds were devastated. Governor Philip Gardelin's Code of 1733 was written primarily as a response to the problem of marooning. Almost half of the nineteen provisions included in the code provided punishments for various forms and aspects of maroonage.

If slaves ran away to another country, or even contemplated, conspired, or attempted to leave the country, the punishment was torture by red-hot pincers at three separate public locations, followed by execution.

Those running away or conspiring to run away from the plantation, but not involving escape from the Danish islands were to lose a leg. If their masters pardoned them, they were to receive 150 strokes and suffer the loss of an ear.

Punishments of varying severity such as the cutting off of a leg, branding or whipping were prescribed for different degrees of maroonage, such as maroonage lasting over six months, maroonage over two weeks, and failure to inform of plots to run away.

The outnumbered whites also felt it necessary to include in the code, punishments for failure to show proper respect and deference. Menacing gestures or verbal insults to whites could be punishable by hanging, preceded by three applications of glowing pincers. At the discretion of the insulted or menaced victim, the slave's punishment could alternatively be the amputation of an arm. If a slave met a white person on the street, the slave would have to step aside.

It was prohibited for slaves to wear iron-tipped sticks or knives at their sides, although the carrying of machetes was allowed. The reason for this was that because the slaves were prohibited from owning weapons, they had developed the art of fighting with their walking sticks. This form of fighting reached the sophistication of the advanced martial arts practiced in other areas of the world. Machetes, on the other hand, were perceived as tools.

Theft of property by slaves was punishable by torture followed by hanging. Petty theft and possession of stolen property was punishable by branding on the forehead and up to 150 strokes.

Being out past curfew was punishable by whipping. Dancing, feasts, or funeral rites involving the use of "Negro instruments" as well as the practice of Obeah was prohibited and would be punished by whipping.

Conspiracy to poison, or the use of poison, was punishable by torture with hot pincers, being broken on the wheel and then burnt alive.

The preamble to the code expressed the philosophy that the slave was the property of the owner and had no rights.

The law was written in an effort to control the slaves through intimidation and terror and, thereby to prevent marooning. The passage of the law, however, produced the opposite effect. The slaves, faced with the impossible choice between starvation on one hand and mutilation and execution on the other, realized that their only way out was rebellion.

Rebellion

On November 23, 1733 slaves carrying bundles of wood were let into the fort at Coral Bay. Concealed in the wood were cane knives, which the rebels used to kill the half-asleep and surprised soldiers who were guarding the fort. One soldier, John Gabriel, escaped by hiding under his bed and running away when he had a chance. He was able to get to St. Thomas in a small boat and tell the story to Danish officials there. The rebels raised the flag and fired three cannon shots. This was the signal for slaves on the plantations to kill their masters and take control of the island.

The rebels proceeded to kill many of the whites in the Coral Bay area. The insurgents gained in number as they progressed from plantation to plantation. Some whites were spared, notably the company's doctor, Cornelius Bödger, because of the good relationship he had with the Africans in treating their medical needs. Also spared were Dr. Bödger's two stepsons. They were saved from death out of respect for the surgeon, and also to be made into servants for the new rebel leaders.

The stated aim of the rebels was to make St. John an Akwamu ruled state, governed under the Akwamu system. Africans of other tribal origins were to serve as slaves in the production of sugar and other crops.

Many of the small planters on the East End, who had few slaves or possessions, were able to escape to other islands in their family boats. Some of the whites from the western and southern parts of the island were warned by loyal slaves, and they were either able to escape to St. Thomas or to assemble with the other surviving planters at Durloe's Plantation at Caneel Bay (then known as Klein Caneel Bay). The approach to the plantation was guarded in part by two cannons. Captain Jannis von Beverhaut and Lt. Charles assumed command. Women and children were sent to Henley Cay with the intention that they be picked up later and brought to St. Thomas.

Meanwhile, the rebels attacked Cinnamon Bay (then called Caneel Bay). John and Lieven Jansen and a small group of their slaves resisted the onslaught. The rebel force was overwhelming. Jansen's loyal slaves fought a rear guard action and held off the advancing rebels with gunfire, thus allowing the Jansens to retreat to their waiting boat and escape to Durloe's Plantation. Miraculously, the loyal slaves were also able to escape.

The rebels paused to loot the Jansen plantation before pressing onward to confront the white planters at Durloe's. The attackers became disorganized when faced with the initial cannon and musket fire of the defenders, and the attack on Durloe's plantation was repulsed.

Meanwhile in St. Thomas, Governor Philip Gardelin, under pressure from former Governor Moth, consented to send a small party of soldiers to St. John to relieve the besieged planters. More troops under the leadership of William Barrens, as well as a detachment consisting mainly of African slaves sent by the Danish West India Company and by St. Thomas planters, arrived on St. John soon afterwards. This well-armed and well-supplied army was able to recapture the fort and scatter the rebels who then took to hiding in the bush to fight a war of attrition.

To regain the status quo, the planters needed to wipe out the last vestiges of resistance. The remaining rebels could continue to survive by looting abandoned plantations and small farms and by living off the land where cattle now ran wild all over the island. The rebels would be a constant harassment to the orderly development and operation of any restored plantations. Furthermore, the Company and the St. Thomas planters feared that the St. John rebellion would inspire uprisings on St. Thomas and wanted to discourage slaves on that island from taking similar action.

The insurgents held their ground, fighting a guerrilla style war and disappearing into the bush when confronted with direct attack by the numerically superior troops led by the planters. This status quo continued for ten weeks.

The British were also concerned that the rebellion might spread to Tortola, and they decided to help the Danes by sending an English Man O' War from Tortola to St. John. The warship was commanded by a Captain Tallard had a crew of sixty soldiers.

When the British ship landed on St. John, the rebels staged an ambush in which four of Tallard's men were wounded. Tallard and his men, demoralized by this defeat, sailed back to Tortola.

Meanwhile, the owner of the plantation at Maho Bay, William Vessuup, had abandoned his plantation and fled to Tortola after being implicated in a murder. Maroon slaves had taken up residence at his plantation and had later used it as a headquarters for their troops in the rebellion.

In an attempt to regain favor with the Danes and be exonerated from the criminal charges against him, Vessuup offered a plan to trick the rebels. He was to lure the leaders aboard his ship with the promise of supplying them with badly needed guns and ammunition. He then planned to capture the rebel leaders and turn them over to the Danes. This attempt at treachery, however, proved to be unsuccessful.

In February of 1734 the St. John planters again solicited aid from the English, and shortly afterwards Captain John Maddox, a privateer, sailing from St. Christopher (St. Kitts) arrived on the ship Diamond with 50 volunteers. His motivation was personal gain. He arranged a contract with Danish officials that would have allowed him to keep all rebel slaves captured except for the 10 considered most dangerous. They were to be turned over to the Danes for punishment. For these 10 he demanded a payment of 20 pieces-of-eight each. On their first confrontation with the Africans, the forces of John Maddox suffered a loss of three killed (including one of his sons) and five wounded. Like his predecessor Captain Tollard, Captain Maddox and his men left St. John shortly after their defeat.

English Governor Mathews wrote:

> On St. John the Danes at present hardly have possession. Their negroes rose upon them about six months ago. At my first arrival I heard they had quelled their slaves, but it was not so, they have in a manner drove the Danes off, at least they dare not now attempt any more to reduce these Negroes, who have always beaten them, and in a manner are masters of that Island. The governor of St. Thomas, was even modest enough to desire I would send some of H. M. ships to reduce them...and I now learn a rash fellow from St. Christophers, in open defiance of my positive orders to the contrary, having made a compact with the Danish governor, went with his two sons and three or four and twenty more on this errand, that the negroes have killed one if not both his sons, and two or three more of his company, and beaten them off.

In early April of 1734 a group of about forty rebels attacked Durloe's Plantation. This assault, like the previous one, was almost successful, but was finally repulsed by the defenders. The insurgents managed, though, to set fire to the defenders supply magazine.

Events in far away Europe were to deal a deathblow to the rebel cause. King Louis of France wanted to make his father-in-law, Stanislas Leszcynski the King of Poland. This would mean war with Poland, and France needed to know that Denmark would at least stay neutral. In addition to this, France was in need of money after having suffered severe financial losses in their Mississippi colony.

The Danes had been interested in the island of St. Croix for quite some time. Sensing an opportunity, the Danish West India Company offered the French 750,000 livres for St. Croix and sweetened the deal with the promise of Danish neutrality.

As a gesture of solidarity with their new friends, France offered Denmark help in subduing the slave rebellion on St. John. Monsieur de Champigny, the Governor of the French West Indies, sent Commander Chevalier de Longueville from Martinique to St. John with a force of two hundred soldiers. This included a free colored corps whose specialty was the tracking down, capturing and killing of runaway slaves, an activity they called maroon hunting.

The French detachment arrived on St. John on April 23, 1734 in two vessels, one commanded by Monsieur de Longueville and the other commanded by Monsieur Nadau. Danish Governor Gardelin dispatched a force of about 30 men under the command of Lt. Froling to offer any assistance necessary to the French soldiers. Gardelin also sent attorney Fries who was to mete out justice to captured rebels.

The French troops proceeded to relentlessly pursue the remaining rebels. A rebel encampment of twenty-six huts was found and destroyed. A young severely wounded slave named January was captured and led the soldiers to a point of land (Ram Head Point) where eleven rebels had committed suicide.

A few weeks later eight slaves, two of whom were women, surrendered after their master promised them clemency.

From *St. John Backtime,* "The Raw Truth has Been Reported," Commander Longueville, from a document discovered and in the Colonies section of the French National Archives by Aimery P. Caron and Arnold R. Highfield:

> On Sunday the 16 (May 16, 1734), six Negroes and two negroe women surrendered at the appeal of their master who spared their lives. He then informed me of the matter. I ordered him to bring them to me, since they were identified as rebels. I have them put into chains. Three of them were burned at the stake on three different plantations on St. John. I had previously informed the governor while passing through St. Thomas that should I catch a few of the rebels, I would put most of them to death and send him the rest so that he could make an example of them. The following day I informed him of their capture. He sent a judge who passed sentence for the sake of formality; I sent him the three other rebels along with the two women and requested that he not have them executed until I be present. One was burned to death slowly, another was sawed in half and the third was impaled. The two Negroe women had their hands and heads cut off after all five had been tortured with hot pincers in the town.
>
> One week later twenty-five rebels were found dead on an "outjutting point of land in an unsuspected place" identified later as near Brown Bay. Commander Longueville and his men left St. John a few days later on May 26, 1744 and sailed to St. Thomas.

Unbeknownst to Longueville at the time of this departure, still at large, but hiding in the bush, was one of the leaders of the rebellion and a small group of his followers. He was a former Akwamu noble who was named Prince by his master. Through an intermediary, a deal was arranged whereby Prince and his supporters would be forgiven and allowed to come back to work.

Prince and fourteen others surrendered to a Sergeant Øttingen. Prince was summarily shot and killed. His head was cut off as a trophy and his followers were captured. Subsequently four of the followers died in jail in St. Thomas, six were tortured to death and four were sent to St. Croix to be worked to death.

Sergeant Øttingen was given a reward and was promoted to Lieutenant for his bravery. The soldiers under him were also honored and rewarded.

The Danish West India Company reported that their losses in this rebellion amounted to 7,905 Rigsbankdalers.

section three

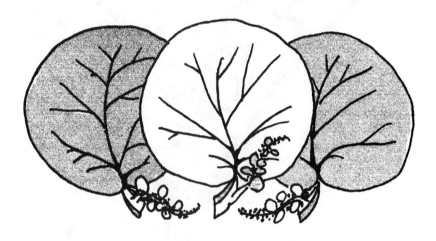

COASTAL ECOLOGY

elkhorn coral

CORAL REEF

The coral reef is the underwater equivalent of the tropical rainforest. Thousands of species of plants and animals live in and around the coral reef. Without coral reefs the tropical seas would be devoid of life. The seagrass beds, the mangroves and all other environments of St. John are dependent upon the coral reef for their existence.

The coral reef, like the rainforest, is not a single entity but a community of plants and animals interacting to form a unique and indispensable environment.

How coral reefs are formed

The basic ingredient of the coral reef is an animal called a coral polyp.

Corals are members of the Phylum Cnidaria (Nigh-DARE-ee-uh). Individual coral polyps can be compared to tiny jellyfish, which are also members of this phylum.

Avoiding the, "Which came first, the chicken or the egg?" question, let us say that the coral reef begins with the larva produced by the sexual reproduction of mature coral polyps. At this stage it will have a soft stomach and tentacles with no hard limestone casing. The tiny larva, along with other plankton, will then drift near the surface of the ocean at the mercy of predators, wind, waves and current.

Only a minute proportion of coral larva will avoid predators and also succeed in coming in contact with a section of ocean substrate that has not yet been colonized by other organisms, and meets the additional requirements of being in warm, clear, properly saline and sufficiently circulated water. If all these condition are met, the larva will attach itself to that spot and become a coral polyp. The polyp then secretes calcium carbonate to form a hard cup around its soft body.

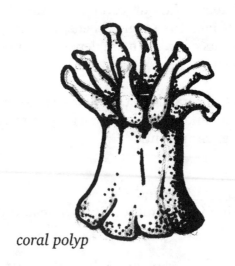

coral polyp

Once the polyp is securely fastened to the substrate and fully armored by a colorful calcium carbonate cup, it begins a process of asexual reproduction. It does this by sending out buds, which form new polyps right beside the parent polyp. Parent and child are cemented together. The process repeats itself, little by little. Coral structures at times hundreds of miles long and thousands of acres in area are formed.

Coral reefs are the largest structures built by any organism on Earth, including man. Some reefs contain more building materials than the largest cities in the world. This is not a rapid process, though, and many reefs are thousands of years old.

Although each polyp is an individual animal, it shares passageways to the stomachs of its parent and offspring. Moreover the polyps within a colony have the ability to act in unison.

Necessary factors for coral reef development

In order for a reef to begin and to continue growing, certain stringent conditions must be met.

A clean place

There must be a firm, clean base for attachment. This can occur on rocky outcroppings on the ocean floor, on top of old coral platforms that are no longer alive, or on human-made structures like wrecks, concrete columns and pipelines.

Water temperature

The next condition is suitable water temperature. In order for the coral to survive the water temperature must consistently be between 70 and 85 degrees Fahrenheit. For optimum growth, however, the water temperature needs to be in an even narrower range, which is between 75 and 80 degrees Fahrenheit. This limits the area where reefs can survive to a narrow band of ocean about one thousand miles north and south of the equator.

Salinity

Proper salinity is another condition. Water salinity must be between 30 and 36 parts per thousand. The ocean average is 35 parts per thousand, so under normal circumstances the correct salinity can be found. However, factors such as the presence of large freshwater rivers flowing into the ocean, runoff from land development, or a prolonged series of extremely low tides can bring the water salinity to unacceptable levels.

Water circulation

Water movement over the reef is yet another condition for the coral's healthy and continuing existence. Waves or currents are necessary to bring plankton past the waiting tentacles of the coral polyps and to renew the supply of oxygen in the water. Water motion also serves the important task of removing waste products, such as sand, from the reef, which would otherwise suffocate the living coral. This process is also of the utmost importance in the creation and maintenance of our beautiful St. John beaches. This requirement of proper water movement explains why reefs are most often found around headlands and in well-flushed bays.

Water clarity

The coral polyp generally feeds at night by catching plankton with its stinging tentacles and sticky holding cells. The throat of the polyp has ciliated cells, which create water currents sending tiny plankton and other fine particles into the stomach. The polyp is efficient at trapping just about all the plankton that comes its way. This usually provides just about enough energy for the coral to survive, but not nearly enough for it to continue building more reefs.

Over 80% of the energy spent by the polyp comes from a symbiotic relationship that it has with microscopic brown algae called zooxanthellae (zo-zan-THEL-ee). This algae lives in the body of the coral polyp where it is provided with a place to live and excellent protection against enemies.

The zooxanthellae provide nourishment for the coral. They produce food through the process of photosynthesis and share this nourishment with the coral polyp. Since photosynthesis requires sunlight, coral reefs are only found in relatively shallow water where light is able to penetrate. This is also the reason that many coral structures resemble plants. Like plants, they branch out maximizing their exposure to the sun.

In addition, Zooxanthellae excrete substances that lower the acidity levels within the polyps. This enables the coral to produce the calcium carbonate for reef building at a much faster pace. The zooxanthellae algae also give corals their color. Some years ago in the Caribbean there was a phenomena called coral bleaching. The zooxanthellae algae were dying, causing the coral to turn white and die.

The condition of water clarity is particularly dependent on the presence of plankton. Floating and swimming about the surface of the world's oceans are small, sometimes microscopic, plants and animals called plankton. Some larger plankton can be seen with the naked eye. If you look carefully at the water about you, when snorkeling or scuba diving, you will see tiny particles suspended in the water. These particles are plankton.

Plankton provide food for all other life in the ocean. Plant plankton, called phytoplankton, produce more oxygen than any other source on our planet. Phytoplankton are dependent on sunlight for the process of photosynthesis to take place. They need to be near the surface of the ocean where there is more sunlight. The animal plankton, called zooplankton, depend primarily on the phytoplankton for food. They are generally found immediately below the level of plant plankton.

In colder parts of the world the ocean water is warmer on the bottom than on top, especially in the winter. Nutrients washed down from the land by rivers, as well as waste products of fish and other sea life, tend to settle towards the bottom. Warm water rises, and because the bottom of the sea is warmer than the top, the nutrients are swept towards the surface by rising currents. These nutrients act as fertilizer for the phytoplankton, and also may serve as food for the zooplankton. The presence of these nutrients near the ocean surface causes there to be an abundance of planktonic life. There is so much plankton in these colder areas that the water appears murky.

In tropical areas the sun warms the ocean. It does not get cold in winter, so the water closer to the surface is warmer than the water closer to the bottom. There are few upward currents. Nutrients tend to settle to the bottom and stay there. Planktonic life is scarce, and the warm waters of the tropics are consequently quite clear. This is another reason why reefs are only found in tropical waters, and why they provide an oasis of life in an otherwise lifeless sea.

Enemies of the coral reef

There is a constant natural process of reef degeneration and regrowth. The force of waves over the reef can break off sections of coral. Parrotfish bite at the reef looking for algae and may break off small pieces. Hurricanes can cause major damage to the reef and the surrounding environment. Meanwhile the reef is constantly rebuilding itself through a slow process of asexual reproduction. As long as these factors stay in balance, the reef will survive.

Humans can exert certain pressures on the reef, which, unlike natural phenomena, can be, not only severe, but also continual. These forces generally cause damage more quickly than the reef's ability to regenerate.

The greatest human-made problem is turbidity, or water cloudiness. On St. John there are many roads that have never been paved. During hard rains water flows over and down these roads picking up great quantities of soil and sediment. These sediments eventually wash into the sea, making the water cloudy and limiting the ability of the symbiotic algae to produce food for the coral animal. Excavation for houses and other buildings can cause the same problem, especially when proper retaining walls and silt fences are not employed quickly enough to prevent erosion, or when disturbed land is not immediately replanted.

Salt ponds, mangrove swamps, and undersea grasslands, which control turbidity by trapping sediment washed down from the land, are also under pressure from humans. Mangrove swamps are cut down and filled, salt ponds are drained or opened to the sea, and undersea grasslands are destroyed by boats anchoring in seagrass beds. The result is more turbidity and reef damage.

This is a vicious cycle. The seagrass and mangroves need calm water in order to grow. The reef protects the shoreline from the full force of the ocean waves. If the reef is damaged it provides less protection for the seagrass and mangroves. Less seagrass and mangroves means more turbidity. More turbidity means more pressure on the reef.

Humans may also interfere with the natural levels of salinity and water temperature. Desalination plants, placed too close to the reef, can cause water temperature and salinity to rise to unacceptable levels with resultant reef damage. Fertilizer runoff and industrial waste discharge can have the same effect.

Chemical waste pollution can quickly kill the delicate reef, and improper sewage treatment can cause the proliferation of seaweed and other algae that can smother the coral and colonize areas upon which polyps would ordinarily grow. Improper disposal of garbage can also be a problem. Something as simple as a plastic bag can smother coral as well as kill turtles and other marine life.

Another problem is the influx of thousands of tourists each year and an exponential increase in the recreational use of the near shore waters. Irresponsible boating, snorkeling and diving can cause major damage to coral. Boats colliding with or running aground upon reefs can destroy large sections of living coral. Anchors set in the reef can break off pieces of coral, and anchors set in sand but near the reef can cause problems if the anchor chain or line sweeps over coral formations. Snorkelers and divers can also adversely impact the reef. Just lightly touching live coral can damage the surface mucus layer of the coral animal, making the polyp more susceptible to infection. Worse yet, is when snorkelers inadvertently kick the coral with their fins or actually stand on the living coral reef when they get tired or frightened.

SEAGRASS

Local seagrass species include shoal grass, turtle grass and manatee grass. These underwater grasses are commonly found on the sandy bottoms of calm bays and between coral reefs. They reproduce and grow by means of an underground root called a rhizome, which lies down horizontally just beneath the sand. From this rhizome the blades of grass grow up and the roots grow down, forming a mat of root fibers that hold the seagrass to the ocean floor. Seagrass is dependent on sunlight and therefore, cannot tolerate cloudy water for extended periods of time.

Seagrasses control erosion by holding down loose sandy soils with their mat of roots, thus protecting our beautiful beaches. Moreover, they help prevent turbidity, or water cloudiness. This is an important function because cloudy water blocks out sunlight. One organism that is extremely sensitive to turbidity is the coral polyp, which is the building block of the coral reef. Although coral polyps are animals, most of their energy comes from a symbiotic relationship with algae that live within the cup-shaped opening of the polyp. Because algae are plants, they will die without adequate sunlight. Without the symbiotic algae, the coral polyp cannot survive, and without the coral polyp there can be no coral reef community.

Seagrasses control turbidity by trapping sediments washed down from land during rains and ultimately incorporating them into a seabed soil that is held securely by the seagrass roots. The blades of grass also slow down bottom currents and keep loose sediments from getting churned up.

Seagrass beds support a great deal of marine life. They provide nutrition for the green turtle and queen conch, and serve as a

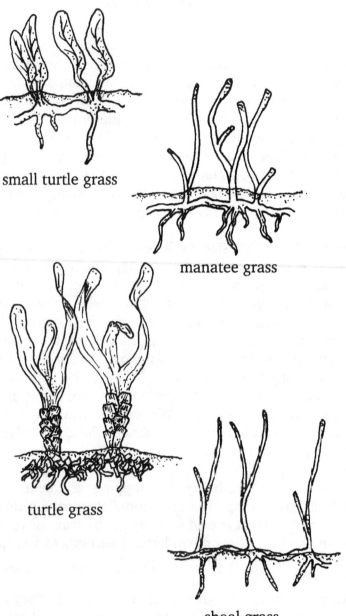

small turtle grass

manatee grass

turtle grass

shoal grass

habitat for many species of juvenile fish and other sea creatures that are small enough to hide between the blades of grass.

Although not quite as sensitive as corals, seagrasses are also threatened by turbidity. They are currently in grave danger from the exponential increase in residential and commercial development on St. John. The prime turbidity-causing culprit is the failure to pave roads. Other enemies of clear water include unprotected and irresponsible excavation, especially on steep slopes, and improper sewage treatment.

A more immediate threat to seagrass comes from the proliferation of boat anchoring. The act of setting down and then pulling up an anchor tears the seagrass up by the roots and destroys the rhizomes, making recovery slow and difficult. Worse yet, when anchors are set improperly, they may drag, causing widespread damage that often includes injury to nearby coral reefs. Moreover, as an anchored boat swings around in the wind, the anchor chain is dragged over the sea floor in an arc, destroying all the grass in its path.

Years ago, harbors such as Caneel, Maho and Francis Bays had extensive seagrass cover. In those days literally hundreds of conch ambled slowly through the seagrass leaves at the bottom of the bays. With the advent of modern tourism and the great increase in the number of boats anchoring in these picturesque and well-protected harbors, the seagrass has all but disappeared and the conch population has plummeted.

Today mariners enjoying many of the most popular bays in St. John may secure their vessels to moorings as an alternative to anchoring. This extensive (and expensive) project was funded by philanthropist, Donald Sussman, in conjunction with the Friends of the National Park and the Virgin Islands National Park. The purpose of the program is the preservation, protection, and hopefully, the revitalization of the seagrass beds that lie on the bottom of these bays.

The current mooring program is a powerful step towards the preservation of seagrass and coral reefs. Unlike anchors, moorings are relatively permanent fixtures. This minimizes the disruption of the seabed. Moreover, moorings do not depend on heavy chains lying on the sea bottom for a secure bite, nor are they subject to dragging.

Hopefully, in addition to the mooring project, future development of St. John will be conducted in an environmentally responsible manner, keeping the bays as clear and as free from turbidity as possible.

Seagrasses tend to be resilient. If the stresses to their survival can be eliminated before it is too late, there is an excellent possibility that our once extensive fields of underwater grasslands will recover fully and will flourish as they did in the past.

MANGROVES

Ecological environments everywhere depend upon one another for their survival. This is elegantly and plainly illustrated in the mangrove habitats of St. John as they quietly preside over the orderly transition of life between land and sea.

The term mangrove loosely describes those tropical trees or shrubs that are specially adapted to grow in salty, wet and muddy environments, such as the shallow waters of calm bays, the periphery of salt ponds, and within marshes and wetlands that are exposed to flooding and salt water intrusion. This is an extraordinary adaptation. Salt is generally abhorrent to plants of any variety. For example, when Union Civil War General William T. Sherman made his infamous "march to the sea", he salted the fields of southern farmers, thus destroying the crops and rendering the farms useless for years to come. Mangroves not only have to withstand the rigors of a saltwater environment, but they also have to be able to hold firm in the loose and oxygen-poor soils characteristic of these locations.

The red mangrove proliferates along the shorelines of shallow calm bays, both on the muddy shore and in the water itself. The red is the classic mangrove characterized by its numerous arch-shaped roots that start at the base of the tree and arch out and down into the water and mud. It also has distinctive seeds that at maturity look something like foot-long red pencils, which emerge prominently from the center of the mangrove's leaf clusters.

When the red mangrove seedling matures, it falls from the tree into the water. Here, it can stay alive and afloat for up to a year. As the seedling moves at the mercy of the winds and currents, it

begins to develop. Tiny side roots emerge from one end of the seed and small leaves on the other. The root end of the seed absorbs water and becomes heavier than the leaf end. The added weight tips the long seed, turning it leaf end up and root end down.

In order to survive and begin to reproduce, the root end of the seed needs to reach shallow enough water so as to obtain at least a tenuous foothold in the mud. Then it must enjoy calm enough water conditions so that it will not be moved until its roots have a chance to secure themselves to the soil. To achieve these conditions the mangrove is dependent on the marine environments of the coral reef and underwater grasslands as well as upon the geography of the region.

The sticky mud that serves to catch the root end of the seed is a mixture of dirt, organic debris that is washed down to the bay from land during heavy rains, and sand, which is a product of the coral reef. The sediments and organic material provide nutrients and stickiness while the sand provides stability and substance for the mixture.

The necessary ultra-calm water conditions are also produced by a combination of environmental factors. In the Virgin Islands, bays are formed at the bottoms of valleys by the mountain ridges that line the sides of the valleys. These ridges extend further out to sea than the center of the valley and form the rocky headlands that we call points. The headlands protect the bay from the full force of the ocean. Coral reefs, growing along the edges of the headlands where the bay is open to the sea, provide an effective barrier against waves and currents. Seagrass beds growing within the center of the bay further calm the water. The numerous blades of grass present a large surface area through which bottom currents must pass, thus slowing them considerably. The proper combination of all these environments may result in a body of water so tranquil that barely a ripple can be seen for days at a time - conditions quiet enough to allow the red mangrove's pencil-sized seed the time it needs to root and mature.

Observing the developments of the mangrove seedling, we can see how much the mangrove depends upon its neighboring terrestrial and marine environments to reproduce. Correspondingly, these environments also depend on the mature mangrove for their survival.

Once its seedling is firmly rooted, the mangrove grows rapidly, achieving as much as three feet in height within the first year. Around the third year it develops the arch-shaped roots that are so distinctive of its species. These are called aerial prop roots - "aerial" because, although the bottoms of the roots go through the water and stick in the mud, much of the root is above the surface of the water, or in the air, and "prop" because they prop up, or support, the mangrove. The aerial prop roots grow to form an arch, which is one of the strongest architectural supports. These roots are so strong, that even though they usually measure less than an inch in diameter, you can walk on top of them and they won't break. When the mangrove gets older and larger, it also sends out drop roots, which descend from the branches. Although the mangrove grows in loose and muddy soil, these two types of roots, acting together, anchor the mangroves so securely that they serve as an effective deterrent to coastline damage even during severe hurricanes.

In addition to preserving the coastline, mangroves promote the health of the coral reef and seagrass beds by protecting them against their most insidious enemy, turbidity or water cloudiness. During heavy rains, water flows down the slopes of mountain valleys into rocky streambeds that we call guts. The guts channel the water directly into the sea or sometimes into marshes and salt ponds near the coast. The water carries earth, pebbles, organic debris, like old dead leaves and twigs, and whatever else is in the way of the stream. This is a potential problem because this debris-laden water, called runoff, can make the seawater turbid and coral reefs and seagrass cannot long survive in cloudy water.

Here, mangroves come to the rescue. Their roots act like a filter, trapping the runoff debris within their thick and tangled web. This prevents the sediment-laden runoff from flowing directly into the ocean where it would cause widespread turbidity and reef damage. Moreover, the mangrove turns this potential problem into a vital resource. The runoff organic matter meets up with literally tons of mangrove leaves that have fallen in the water. Trapped within the tangle of mangrove roots, this organic stew is broken down by microorganisms and turned into suitable food for other creatures that feast on the rotting debris as well as upon the microorganisms themselves. Thus, the underwater mangrove forest becomes a world in itself, providing a rich and plentiful habitat for countless species of baby fish and tiny sea creatures that also find sanctuary amidst the intricate maze of protective roots.

Another interesting result of the debris-filtering nature of mangrove roots is that not only do they prevent loss of land due to coastal erosion, but they also actually cause the shoreline to expand thereby creating more land. As the trapped sediments and debris are broken down and stabilized, they build up and gradually rise above the surface of the water. This new dry land will eventually be colonized by other plant species that, although not as salt-tolerant as the red mangrove, are better suited for life on dry land. The red mangrove responds to this inland competition by simply moving farther out to sea, and little by little the size of our island increases.

In these numerous ways, mangroves are truly guardians of the shoreline. They protect the coast from erosion and hurricanes, the coral reef and the seagrass beds from turbidity, the tiny sea creatures from large predators, and turn potentially harmful runoff into essential nutrients for the marine community and into solid land for the expansion of St. John.

SALT PONDS

How important are St. John's salt ponds? The complex balance of land and sea environments supports the incredible natural beauty of St. John, the white soft sandy beaches, the crystal-clear water, the colorful coral reef, the fish, the sea creatures, the exotic tropical foliage, the birds, bats, butterflies and every other living thing. One of these environments that is often over-looked is the salt pond.

Most of the salt ponds of St. John were once bays, open to the sea. Coral reefs develop naturally around the rocky headlands that jut out and define bays. In time the reef may extend out from the headland toward the center of the bay. When this happens simultaneously on both headlands, the bay begins to be closed off. As the reef matures, the top of the reef rises toward the surface of the water. Severe storms or hurricanes may carry sand, rocks and pieces of broken coral and pile them on top of the reef creating a surface platform above sea level. Meanwhile heavy rains and gut washes cause sediments and soil from the land to collect on the protected side of the platform facing the land. With the help of salt tolerant plants, such as mangroves, to secure these sediments, the platform will gradually get larger and denser. A salt pond is born when the spit of solid land builds up enough to close off the bay from the sea.

During heavy rains, water runs down valleys and hillsides into guts, which in turn lead to the low flat areas just inshore from the central portions of the bay. Salt ponds are generally found in these low-lying areas and serve as a buffer between land and sea. The water flowing down the valley picks up soil, organic debris and possibly dangerous pollutants. This mix is deposited into the salt pond instead of washing directly into the sea. The sediments settle to the bottom of the pond and the now purified water can seep through the filter-like sand and coral rubble wall of the pond into the bay without causing turbidity or cloudiness. Turbidity, as we know, is the greatest enemy of the coral reef, which provides protection for our coastline from the full force of ocean waves, sand for our beaches and serves as a habitat for the great majority of the fish and sea creatures in our area.

Salt ponds are extremely hostile environments for living things. Depending on the salt pond's location and on conditions such as temperature, rainfall and windiness, the water within the pond can range from almost fresh to a super-saline solution five times the saltiness of the sea. Add to this the high temperature that the water can reach during sunny dry afternoons and you would think that nothing could survive there. Nonetheless, the salt pond is inhabited by such creatures as brine shrimp, crabs, insects and insect larva, which provide the basis for a food chain. Birds, waterfowl and bats that feed on these organisms are attracted to the pond environment and several species of birds tend to make their nests nearby.

Birds commonly found at or near St. John salt ponds include herons, sandpipers, yellowlegs, and pin tail ducks. In addition, certain fish, such as barracuda, tarpon, mullet and snook, attracted by the brine shrimp, sometimes make their way into salt ponds that have an opening to the sea. In some parts of the world the brine shrimp from salt ponds are harvested commercially for tropical fish food, and the larva produced by brine shrimp eggs has been marketed (particularly in comic books) as "sea monkeys".

Salt ponds can be smelly and murky and in the past they were indiscriminately dredged, drained, filled or opened to the sea. As a result they have been disappearing from the Virgin Islands at an alarming rate. Fortunately, they are now protected under the territorial Coastal Zone Management department and also under federal legislation, which means no filling, opening or dredging.

If you would like to observe a St. John salt pond, the best time to visit is in the early morning, while it is still cool. The morning is also the best time to bird watch at the ponds. Some easily accessible and healthy pond environments can be found at Frank, Europa, Grootpan and Salt Pond Bays. Salt ponds tend to be peaceful and quiet areas. Take your time, stand still and look about carefully; you'll be pleasantly surprised at all there is to see and contemplate.

BEACHES

There are three general classifications of beaches on St. John. The most beautiful and most popular are the soft white coral sand beaches typically found within the National Park on St. John's north shore. Sand beaches like these are found in areas where the water offshore is relatively shallow, the depth drops off gradually and the coral reefs and headlands are strategically located. The sand is produced as a waste product of the reef community and is deposited on the shore by the action of waves.

A coral rubble beach is formed on shorelines where the reefs are deeper, the bottom drops off more rapidly, and wave energy is higher and more constant. Broken up pieces of coral are washed ashore instead of sand. An example of this type of beach is Europa Bay within Lameshur Bay.

The third type of beach is the cobblestone beach. These beaches are also found where there is deeper reef and higher wave action, but, due to the dynamics of the placement of the coral reefs and direction of the incoming waves, coral rubble is not washed ashore. These beaches are covered by rocks that originally came from land and have been broken down, rounded and polished by the continual action of waves. These beautiful and colorful cobblestones often make a hypnotic and musical sound as they roll about in the waves. Examples of cobblestone beaches are Great Lameshur Bay and Klein Bay.

Where does the sand come from?
The satiny soft coral sand found on the majority of St. John's beaches comes, almost entirely, from the coral reef community.

Reef grazing fish, such as parrotfish, produce a significant amount of the sand found on our beaches. Parrotfish exist on a diet of algae, which they scrape off the surface of coral rock with their fused teeth that look like a parrot's beak. They then grind this coral and algae mixture to a fine powder. The algae covering the coral are absorbed as food. The coral rock passes through their digestive tracts and is excreted in the form of sand. Snorkelers will frequently observe this process if they watch the parrotfish for a few minutes. Scientists say that for each acre of reef a ton of sand is produced by reef grazing fish every year.

Sand is also produced as the coral reef is broken down by wave action. Broken up skeletons of calcareous algae, mollusk shells and sea urchin spines make up more of the sand supply. Only a small proportion of the beach sand is made up of the fine powdered particles that result from the weathering of terrestrial rocks.

How does sand get to the beach?
Sand is basically a waste product of the coral reef. This waste, which would otherwise suffocate the coral, is removed by the action of waves and currents over the reef. The sand is removed to an area around the perimeter of the reef where it collects over time.

During the winter large swells are generated by storms and cold fronts coming from North America and from over the central Atlantic. When these swells reach the north shore of St. John they become steeper and break on the shore. The sand is moved from the storage areas around the reef and deposited on the beach.

In the summer the same process can occur on the southern coasts, caused by the action of the tradewinds or by tropical storms or hurricanes coming from the southeast.

How is sand lost from beaches?

The sand beach can only exist when sand production and sand loss are in balance. There are factors, both natural and man-made, that can disturb this balance.

Winds can blow sand past the line of vegetation, and this sand becomes part of the soil behind the tree line. As the sand on the lower beach is washed back and forth by waves it gets smaller and smaller, until it gets so fine that it goes into suspension. It will then be washed back out to sea.

Hurricanes or strong tropical storms are other natural phenomena that could result in sand loss. Large storms may either take away or add sand to existing beaches. They may even create new beaches. However, these storms often destroy large sections of reef, reducing the sand supply for years to come.

Interference of humans in the natural order of nature can cause a more insidious form of beach destruction. Dredging operations remove sand from sand supplies, thus preventing sand from reaching the beaches in times of ground seas or tropical storms. When St. John first began to experience the boom of tourism with the resultant construction of roads and buildings, a great deal of sand was taken from the beaches to make concrete. In those days, not much was known about beach dynamics. As a result, several St. John beaches are considerably smaller and narrower than they used to be. The process of recovery from this interference is extremely slow, and if the dredging or the mining of sand is continual, the sand beach will be replaced by rocky shoreline.

The worst threat to beaches comes from damage to the coral reef. Remember that all sand found on St. John's beaches comes from the reef, and without a healthy coral reef the beautiful white coral sand beaches of St. John will not continue to exist.

section four

BEACHES AND SNORKELING

SALOMON BAY

If you're a free spirit without a rental car and would rather not depend on a taxi, yet still desire that unbeatable St. John north shore beach experience, Salomon is the beach for you.

Proper attire
In spite of laws to the contrary, it is common to find sunbathers at Salomon Bay with no attire at all. Thus, Salomon has earned the reputation of being a clothing optional beach.

Arrival
There is no road to Salomon. You need to walk the trail (or go by boat). See Map 1, page 269.

From town:
Take the Lind Point Trail, which begins at the National Park Visitors Center in Cruz Bay. It is a little less than one mile to the beach at Salomon Bay.

When you get to the fork in the trail you can go either way. The lower trail is shorter, less hilly, and reaches a maximum elevation of about 100 feet. The upper trail, which climbs to about 150 feet, is a more scenic route as it passes by the Lind Point Overlook.

Shorter walk:
For a shorter walk (a little over a half mile, but with a descent of 250 feet) to Salomon Beach, take the North Shore Road (Route 20) past Mongoose Junction and up the hill. Turn left at the top of the hill where there is a blue Virgin Islands National Park sign. Immediately on the right hand side is a parking area for approximately four vehicles. Park here if you drove. The

Caneel Hill Spur Trail intersects the North Shore Road (Route 20) and is clearly marked with a sign. Take this trail north and downhill to the Lind Point Trail and turn left, then take the first spur trail to the right, which goes down the hill to Salomon Beach.

The View

From Salomon Bay you can see most of the islands that define Pillsbury Sound. Looking from the west to the east you will see St. Thomas, Thatch, Grass, Mingo, Lovango, Ramgoat and Henley Cays and Jost Van Dyke, one of the British Virgin Islands. (The word "cay is pronounced "key" in the Virgin Islands.)

There is a popular but untrue rumor concerning how Lovango Cay got its name. According to the story, there was once a brothel on the island and sailors would "love and go". Actually the names Mingo and Lovango (and Congo which is behind Lovango and cannot be seen from Salomon Bay) were named after sections of Africa from which slaves were brought to the islands.

The three small cays in the middle of the channel between St. John and Lovango, Henley Ram Goat and Rata Cays collectively are called the Durloe Cays after Pieter Durloe the founder of the Klein Caneel Bay Plantation (today called Caneel Bay).

Henley Cay was once known as Women's Cay because during the slave revolt of 1733, surviving white women and children were placed there to await rescue and transportation to St. Thomas. The surviving white men made Durloe's plantation at Caneel Bay their stronghold, which they succeeded in defending against the rebels.

In the 1940s and 1950s Henley, Ramgoat and Rata Cays (The Durloe Cays) were owned by Roger Humphrey, the Marine commandant of the Virgin Islands during World War II. He built the concrete storehouse whose ruins are presently found on Henley Cay. In 1947 Humprey's son, a navy pilot, flew his aircraft over Henley Cay. He apparently was executing some air acrobatics, which he miscalculated, flew too low, crashed into the cay and died. This was the first time a plane had crashed anywhere near St. John. The wreckage of the plane can still be seen on top of the island.

After his son's death Humphrey lost interest in further development of Henley and rarely returned there. In 1948 he rented Henley Cay to Robert and Nancy Gibney, the parents of the present owners of Gibney Beach, who lived there for about a year before building their permanent home at Hawksnest..

Snorkeling

Some of the finest snorkeling on the north shore can be found in the area of the fringing reef that lies around the point separating Salomon and Honeymoon Bay on the northeast corner of Salomon beach.

Most of the reef is in calm shallow water with some sections even rising above the surface at times of extreme low tides, thus snorkelers should make an extra effort to avoid situations where the water is too shallow for them.

The condition of the reef is good, although there has been some damage to the coral caused by irresponsible boating, careless snorkelers, and by natural phenomena, such as heavy ground seas and hurricanes.

The coral reef community here is colorful and diverse. The fish are plentiful, and there is a great deal to see. This is the best-protected and most easily accessible shallow water snorkel in St. John, and it can be thoroughly enjoyed by snorkelers of all experience levels.

Snorkeling in the center of the bay between the fringing reefs, can also be a worthwhile experience. Try to snorkel in areas protected by swim buoys to minimize danger from dinghy traffic in the area.

The sea bottom between the reefs is sand and coral rubble. You will have to look more carefully to find interesting activity, but there really is a great deal of life here. The hills and holes on the sea floor are formed by eels, worms, shrimp, clams and crabs that make their homes on this underwater beach. Meanwhile, you may notice several different varieties of fish swimming about, which are constantly on the lookout for these tasty bottom dwelling seafood dinners.

Snorkeling over the sandy bottom is also a good way for beginners to get practice before attempting to snorkel over reef where there is a possibility of danger to both the snorkeler and to the reef from accidental contact.

Honeymoon Beach

If you would like to experience the excellent snorkeling described for Salomon Bay but prefer a venue offering a more traditional experience in terms of beach attire, Honeymoon Bay is a fine alternative. It lies just to the east of Salomon and enjoys the same natural beauty and fantastic views. The snorkeling reef fringes the rocky point between the two bays and, therefore, is just as easily accessible from either beach.

Honeymoon is accessible from the Caneel Bay Resort or via the Lind Point or Caneel Hill Spur Trails. See Map 1, page 269.

GIBNEY BEACH

Driving east on the North Shore Road (Route 20), about two miles out of town, the entrance to Gibney Beach is marked with an iron gate that reads "Oppenheimer." This marks the entrance to what was once the vacation home of J. Robert Oppenheimer, best known for his work on the atomic bomb. Park at the top and enter through the door in the iron gate and walk down to the beach. The renovated structure that you find at the bottom of

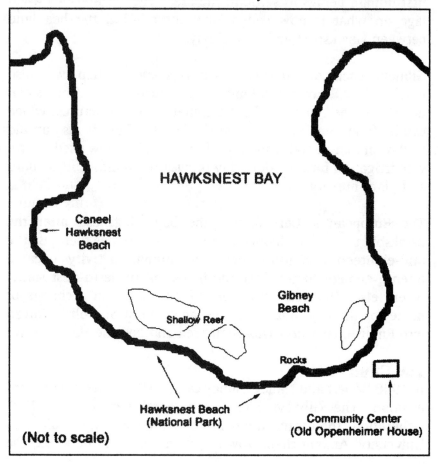

the driveway on the right is the former Oppenheimer home, which is now a Community Center.

The magnificent stretch of white sandy shoreline that you see before you makes a great all day outing with many natural features to explore. You'll enjoy the beach, foliage, reef and fish, rocks and people.

History

Around 1000 AD Amerindian ancestors of the Taino were the first human beings to settle in the area. They established a village on what is now called Hawksnest Point, the headland between Hawksnest and Caneel Bays.

Gibney Beach, or Högsnest, as it was known then, was also inhabited by European colonists and African slaves. This is evidenced by the remains of old colonial period structures, which can be found just inshore from the beach. There is also an old well from that period, which still functions. It is now used to provide irrigation for a modern-day provision ground, fruit orchard and plant nursery.

The European settlers named the bay, Högsnest, after the hawksbill turtle, which once nested on the beaches there. By the mid-eighteenth century, however, human activity became intense enough to convince the hawksbill turtle to nest somewhere else. This fact, however, did not result in a change of name for the bay, but when the language of St. John evolved into English, Högsnest was anglicized and became Hawksnest.

The Gibneys

In 1946 Robert and Nancy Gibney came to St. John on their honeymoon. The Gibneys were an integral part of the "Beat Generation" the center of which was New York City's Columbia University. Among their crowd were the poet, Robert Lax, the painter, Ad Reinherdt, and the author, Thomas Merton.

The Gibneys rented a cottage in Cruz Bay and later leased the home of Julius and Cleome Wadsworth on Denis Bay. In 1949 they moved out to Henley Cay, where they lived in a small building, the remains of which can still be found on the island. (Their friends Lax and Reinherdt visited the Gibneys on Henley Cay and stayed for a summer.)

In 1950 the Gibneys bought a forty-acre parcel on Hawksnest Bay and constructed a house just inland from the center of the beach. They had three children.

The Gibney children followed in their parent's footsteps. Like their father and mother, they were well liked and accepted by the native population and would receive many local visitors. In addition, they attracted a good following of Continentals.

The beat generation evolved into the hippies and when the Gibney children were teenagers they had many friends among the flower children who would often congregate at Hawksnest. Today the tradition continues, and there is still is a definite tendency for Gibney beach to draw an offbeat or "off the beaten track" assembly.

When Robert and Nancy Gibney died, the beach, and the property behind it, was left to their three children and the land was eventually divided amongst them.

Today, the parcel adjoining the old Oppenheimer house, bordered by a white picket fence, is privately owned by the outgoing and gregarious, John and Teri Gibney and their son Tommy.

The parcels of beachfront land belonging to the other two Gibneys were sold to the National Park in 2000, along with the proviso that Eleanor Gibney has the lifetime right to live in the original Gibney house and that Ed Gibney will retain certain rights concerning his parcel.

(A friend of Eleanor Gibney told me, "Eleanor is private and shy - she lives there with her family and dislikes visitors or interruptions, preferring a quiet life.")

Community Center
In 1957 the Gibneys sold a small parcel of their land in Hawksnest to J. Robert Oppenheimer, "the father of the atomic bomb," and his wife, Kitty. The property is at the northeastern extreme of the Gibneys' land, where the Oppenheimers built a vacation home on the beach.

Upon the death of J. Robert Oppenheimer in 1967 and the demise of his widow, Kitty Oppenheimer in 1972, their daughter Toni inherited the property. When Toni died in 1976, she left the property to "the people of St. John for a public park and recreation area."

"The people of St. John" proved to be a nebulous entity and, as no provisions were made for the upkeep of the property, the house and land fell into disrepair. In the 1980s Graffiti covered the walls, and the house was vandalized.

Toni's dream was finally realized in the 1990s when the Virgin Islands Government took charge of the property and created a Community Center there. Today, for a nominal fee, the Center can be rented out for Community functions, such as Senior Citizen outings, Boy Scouts, performances by local Reggae and Calypso bands, picnics, weddings, birthday parties etc.

Snorkeling
Snorkeling is best from the Oppenheimer section of the beach.

The entry into the water is on soft sand and the snorkeling is suitable for beginners.

Enter the water directly in front of the Community Center and begin snorkeling on the shallow reef, which occasionally breaks through the surface of the water.

Much of this reef was harmed when a heavy rain occurred during the excavation for the Myrah Keating Smith Clinic. Tons of earth were washed down into Hawksnest Bay and the resulting turbidity damaged much of the coral in the bay. Today the reefs are coming back to life and you will see some beautiful live elkhorn and boulder coral, along with fire coral and other examples of reef life. Schools of small fish such as, goatfish, grunt and tang can commonly be seen in the area.

A narrow fringing reef runs along the eastern coastline. Close to the beach is a section of beautiful brain coral. The reef here is colorful and there is an abundance of small and medium size fish. Look for parrotfish, angelfish, squirrelfish, trunkfish and trumpetfish. Also, observe the predators such as yellowtail snapper and blue runners prowling the reef edges on the lookout for fry and other small prey.

More experienced snorkelers can continue along this eastern coast to the point and around to Perkins Cay and Denis Bay. Along the way is a small beach where you can stop and rest. Just before you come to this pocket beach you may see the remains of a sunken sailboat. As you progress northward along the coast you will encounter scattered areas of colorful coral, sponges, fish and other marine life in depths of about six to ten feet. Snorkeling here is best in the summer when there are no ground seas to churn up the water.

Beginner Snorkel

On the other side of the bay, the area of large rocks between Hawksnest and Gibney is in shallow water with a sand bottom adjacent to the rocks. Here you will see schools of small fish, grunts, fry and goatfish. Children will especially enjoy this non-threatening environment.

In many places the water is shallow enough to stand on the sand bottom. Look closely at the rocks. You will see sponges, green algae, father duster and Christmas tree worms and small patches of coral. Observe the parrotfish grazing the algae and watch the spunky damselfish defend its territory against any intruders regardless of size.

WHISTLING CAY, MARY POINT AND JOHNSON'S REEF

Kayaks are available for rent at the beach at Cinnamon Bay. Intermediate and advanced snorkelers can access excellent snorkeling at Whistling Cay or Mary's Point. Advanced snorkelers should consider Johnson's Reef.

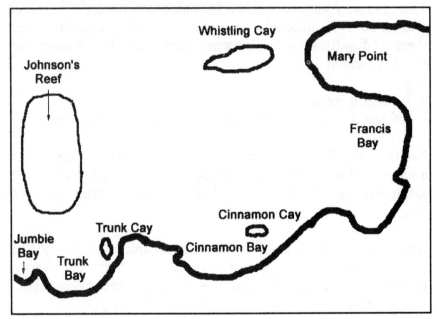

Whistling Cay

At Whistling Cay the kayaks can be put ashore on the pebble beach in the vicinity of the partially restored stone customs house. There are also other small cobblestone beaches on the west side of the island near the mooring buoys. Once your kayak is securely up on dry land, you can enter the water to enjoy the excellent snorkeling all around Whistling Cay, the best of which is in the vicinity of the big rocks off the northwestern point.

Mary Point

At Mary' Point there is a small beach where the kayaks can easily be hauled out of the water. You'll find beautiful snorkeling all along the shoreline of the small passage, called Fungi Passage, between Whistling Cay and St John.

Be careful not to go too far offshore, as there is the ever-present danger of boat traffic in the passage.

This area may also be reached by snorkeling from the beach at Francis Bay, but quite a bit of swim time will be spent in getting there and getting back. For more details see the Francis Bay Snorkel chapter.

Johnson's Reef

If you see the reef breaking, don't go. Wait for a calm day.

Paddle out to the reef and put on your gear. Get out of the kayak and snorkel as you tow the kayak by the bowline. This is the safest and easiest way to experience this rarely seen, splendid location.

Never tie a kayak or any boat to the coral and do not anchor on the reef. Anchoring is not only potentially damaging to this fragile environment, but also insecure. (You may return from your snorkel to find that your kayak has drifted away.)

LITTLE CINNAMON BAY

This beautiful soft sand beach is much less visited than its neighbor to the east, and the sea tends to be calmer and the winds less strong. Little Cinnamon has a more northerly exposure than Cinnamon Bay, which provides longer periods of shade.

The beaches of Cinnamon Bay
There are three beaches within Cinnamon Bay. From east to west they are Cinnamon Bay, Little Cinnamon Bay and Peter Bay. (Peter Bay, the next beach to the west, was the location of a shark liver oil factory in the 1940s. Old-timers say that on some summer days you could smell the aroma of shark liver oil as far away as Caneel Bay. Today Peter Bay is an exclusive and expensive residential development.

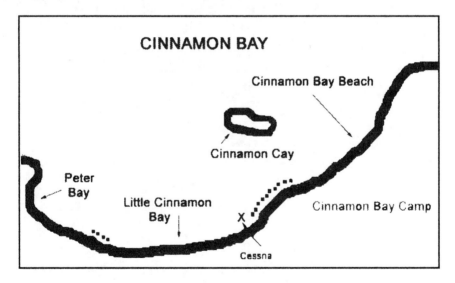

Arrival
First you must get to Cinnamon Bay Campground, which is about four miles east of Mongoose Junction on the North Shore

Road (Route 20). Park in the parking lot and walk to the beach. Go left on the beach and walk to the end where you will pick up a narrow trail that goes through the bush along the shoreline and over a section of rocks, reaching the beach at Little Cinnamon.

Snorkeling

Snorkelers may find the remains of an old Cessna aircraft that crashed and sank years ago. The propeller, the engine and one of the wings are visible most of the year. The wreck is in shallow water and can be found by snorkeling out from the eastern portion of the beach between the old stone wall and the first set of coconut palms.

FRANCIS BAY SNORKEL

Francis Bay can be quite crowded - not with people, but with fish and seabirds.

Large schools of fry often frequent the shallow fringing reef along Francis Bay's rocky north shore. These small silvery fish travel in close proximity to one another in large schools that look like underwater shadows.

On the outskirts of these living clouds, in slightly deeper water, lurk predators, such as jacks, yellowtail snapper, Spanish mackerel, barracuda as well some respectfully-sized tarpon and pompano. Every now and then one of these larger fish will enter to feed, moving quickly into the glittery mass. The fry are extremely sensitive to minute changes in water currents and can sense the approach of the hunters. In a burst of speed they move away from the oncoming predators. Some are successful and some are eaten. Some breach the surface of the water, fly through the air and splash back into the sea. This splash, however, puts them into yet more danger. Waiting pelicans and brown boobies swoop down in the vicinity of the splash scooping up big mouthfuls of tasty fry.

In the midst of all this activity, large schools of French grunts, oblivious to the drama around them, hover, almost motionless, over and around colorful live coral. Parrotfish and blue tang swim about grazing on algae. Little damselfish defend their self-proclaimed territories by darting menacingly at even larger intruders.

A closer look will reveal all sorts of beautiful and mysterious sea creatures like small eels, feather duster and Christmas tree

worms, brightly colored sponges and gracefully swaying gorgonians such as the colorful sea fan.

In the underwater grasslands just seaward of the reef, snorkelers are likely to come upon large green sea turtles often accompanied by stuck-on remora or bar jacks that follow along just
inches above the turtle's back. In this area one may also see
southern stingrays, conch, trunkfish, and others.

Novices who feel more comfortable close to shore can have a
rewarding snorkel around the rocks on the south side of the bay
between Francis and little Maho or over the seagrass that lies in
shallow water on the other end of the beach.

Francis Bay is well worth a visit, so bring your snorkel gear and
join the crowd!

WATERLEMON BAY

Leinster Bay is made up of two smaller bays, Waterlemon Bay on the east and Mary's Creek on the west. To reach Waterlemon Bay, which has two great snorkeling locations, take the Leinster Bay Trail from the parking area at the Annaberg Sugar mill ruins. See Map 4 and 5, pages 272 and 273.

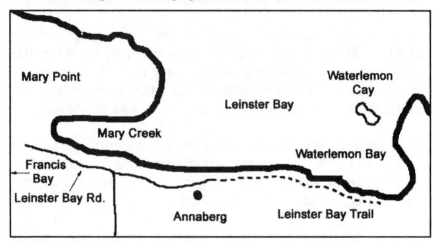

Unnamed beach snorkel

About half way (0.4 mile) down the Leinster Bay Trail, is a small sand and coral rubble beach, which provides excellent snorkeling for intermediate and advanced snorkelers. (This is the first and only sand beach that you pass on the trail before arriving at Waterlemon Beach, a rough sandy beach.)

From the beach enter the water over a shallow area of coral rubble. It is a relatively easy entry, but be careful where you step while putting on your gear to avoid contact with any sea urchins or live coral.

The fringing reef extends out about twenty yards from shore. It is shallow over the top of the reef, but deep enough for experienced and confident snorkelers to negotiate safely. Care should be taken not to kick the coral with your fins. At the seaside edge of the reef is an underwater hillside, which descends about thirty feet to meet the sand and grass bottom of the center portion of the bay.

A good plan is to snorkel west (to the left) over the shallow portion of the reef first and return along the deeper reef edge.

The most abundant corals found in the shallow top reef are colonies of star and boulder coral. There are many small reef fish in the area. You will almost certainly see parrotfish, angelfish, grunts, damselfish and schools of blue tang along with a vast assortment of invertebrates such as sponges and plume worms.

Along the reef edge on the underwater hillside are gardens of sea fans and other gorgonians, sometimes called soft corals. This section of reef tends to attract larger fish such as blue runners, mutton snapper, and yellowtail snapper.

There can be a moderate current here which sets to the west, as well as the possibility of a strong breeze blowing in the same direction. Be prepared for a more difficult return to the beach, as you will be going against the chop and the current.

Waterlemon Cay

Another great spot to snorkel along the Leinster Bay Trail is around Waterlemon Cay, the small island found off the beach at the end of the trail. (Many visitors name this as their favorite snorkel.)

Enter the water from the beach and snorkel over to the island. The water is shallow, and the bottom is coral rubble. It is about a 0.2-mile snorkel to the fringing reef off Waterlemon Cay. The depth between the beach and the island is about twenty-five feet.

Between the St. John shoreline and Waterlemon Cay is an environment of seagrass in about 25 feet of water. On the south and east sides of the island there is shallow water over the top of a fringing reef. On the west and north side of the cay is a beautiful coral reef, which descends to a depth of about twenty feet.

To decrease the snorkeling distance to the island, follow the trail at the far end of the beach. Bear left at the first fork in the trail, which will continue to follow the shoreline. At the end of this trail, walk along the shore and choose a convenient place close to Waterlemon Cay to enter the water. The distance across the channel to the island is only about 0.1 mile. This entry is from the rocky shoreline to a rocky bottom. Be careful not to step on live coral or sea urchins.

From this entry point to the eastern part of Waterlemon Cay, you will snorkel over an area of seagrass and scattered reef. Closer to the island the water becomes quite shallow. Here you will see schools of blue tang and some very large parrotfish. You can hear the parrotfish crunching their beak like teeth along the surface of the rocks and dead coral. They do this to scrape off algae. Chunks of coral and algae pass through the parrotfish's unique digestive system and are excreted as fine coral sand. Much of the sand on our beautiful beaches is produced in this manner.

Around the north and west sides of the island, the underwater seascape is truly an "Octopuses Garden". There are several varieties of hard coral, including excellent specimens of brain coral. Sea fans and sea plumes are found on the deeper parts of the reef. The whole area is alive with a plethora of fish and other sea creatures. Look for eels in holes and for octopus where you find opened seashells piled together signaling a place where they have feasted.

In the seagrass between Waterlemon Cay and the shoreline of St. John you may see starfish, green turtles and stingray.

There is often a current around the island, which is especially strong during new and full moons. If you are not a strong swimmer keep this in mind and proceed with caution. Obviously, it is easier to swim in the direction of the current rather than against it, so choose your direction around the island accordingly.

parrotfish

BROWN BAY

When you are out hiking the trails, Brown Bay Beach is a perfect place to cool off, relax, take a swim and explore the ruins. There are shady places to sit, and usually a cooling ocean breeze. This is a great spot to enjoy a picnic lunch in a natural and private setting.

Arrival

Starting from the Coral Bay Moravian Church, go east about a mile on the East End Road (Route 10.) After you pass Estate Zootenvaal, you will cross a small concrete bridge. Turn left just after the bridge and park on the dirt road. Twenty yards up the road you will come to a fork. As Yogi Berra, the famous baseball player, once said, "When you get to the fork in the road, take it!" The right fork is the beginning of the Brown Bay Trail. It is a three-quarter mile hike to the beach. See Maps 3 and 4, pages 272 and 273.

Brown Bay's white sand beach is almost certain to be deserted as there is no vehicle access and the trail entrance is far from the more populated areas of the island. Also, Brown Bay is a poor anchorage for vessels coming by sea, so it is uncommon to see yachts at anchor here. Enjoy having this idyllic spot all to yourselves.

Snorkeling

The bottom of the bay is sand and grass, offering an easy entry. It is quite shallow at first, but deepens gradually providing access to excellent snorkeling further out from the beach. The snorkeling here is best on calm days when the water is not churned up and murky.

The most colorful and interesting area to snorkel in Brown Bay is around the point on the eastern side of the bay where there is a relatively shallow fringing reef, which slopes down to a depth of about twenty feet. There are several beautiful specimens of hard corals near the top of the reef, and on the sloping hillside is a garden of gorgonians, such as sea fans, sea whips and sea plumes. You will often see larger fish here due to the proximity of the deep Sir Francis Drake Channel.

While snorkeling over the grassy center of the bay, look for green turtles, conch and stingrays.

MANGROVE SNORKELING
PRINCESS BAY

Starting from the intersection of Centerline Road (Routes 10) and Salt Pond Road (Route 107), near the Coral Bay Moravian Church, proceed east 1.8 miles on the East End Road (Route 10) to the mangrove-lined Princess Bay. The bay is close to the road. There is an opening through the mangroves in the center of the bay where a mooring slip for a small boat was once cut out. The slip is a convenient entry point for snorkelers.

Once in the water head east (left), where the mangrove roots grow in water deep enough to comfortably accommodate snorkeling.

Mangrove fringe forests

The prospect of snorkeling in the mangroves is not often greeted with enthusiasm. Mangroves are easily thought of as hot, buggy, smelly swamps. This assessment is essentially correct for *mangrove basin forests* found in the Virgin Islands. These occur where mountain guts flow into large flatlands bordered by shallow well-protected bays. Mangrove basin forests can be hot and muggy, with little breeze and lots of insects. Moreover, the abundance of decaying organic matter in the swamp sends off a decidedly disagreeable odor. Snorkeling the basin forest mangroves is not particularly inviting.

Another type of mangrove habitat, called a *fringe forest*, can also be found in the Virgin Islands. In a fringe forest, mangroves grow along a narrow, partially submerged shelf situated between a well-protected bay and sharply rising hillsides. Because these mangroves are confined to a narrow shelf of land, there are no extensive wetlands and less organic debris, hence the fringe forest is far less humid, supports less insect life, and is not foul smelling like the basin forest. Here, snorkelers can comfortably observe the utterly fantastic underwater nursery for the baby fish that exists only in the mangroves.

Mangrove sea life
Snorkel right up to the mangroves and taking care not to kick up sediment, look inside the tangle of roots. You will be astounded by this vast nursery for tiny fish, such as miniature, blue tang, French grunts, yellowtail snapper, butterfly fish, jacks, damselfish, sergeant majors, parrotfish, old wife, fry and barracuda. The dense, shallow environment of the mangrove roots offers an exceptionally wide variety of baby fish safety from the appetites of larger fish as well as a thick soup of nutrients provided by the decay of mangrove leaves and twigs.

The more you look, the more you'll see - small colorful corals and sponges encrusted to the mangrove roots, oysters, baby lobsters, shrimp, crabs, sea cucumbers, sea urchins and conchs. You may find it amusing to observe the tiny barracudas, some just an inch or two long, exhibiting the same fierce behavior as their larger counterparts, lying almost motionless in the water waiting for the opportunity to dart out and devour fish even tinier than themselves.

Spaghetti worms
The long white strands that look like thread or thin spaghetti belong to a class of tubeworms aptly named spaghetti worms. Gently touch the strand and it withdraws slowly back into its tube.

Upsidedown jellyfish
Another strange creature that inhabits the underwater mangrove environment is the upsidedown jellyfish. These creatures are in the same family as corals and exhibit many of the same traits.

The upsidedown jellyfish supplements its diet of whatever it can trap within its tentacles with food produced through photosynthesis by single-celled algae that have a symbiotic relationship with the jellyfish. As compensation for sharing their food, the algae are allowed to live, secure from danger, inside the poisonous tentacles of the jellyfish. The upsidedown jellyfish spends most of its life lying upside-down on the bottom of mangrove lagoons, allowing the algae to get sunlight.

The scientific name of the upsidedown jellyfish is Cassiopeia frondosa. Virginia Barlow in her excellent book, *The Nature of the Islands*, gives this explanation of the origin of the name:

> Cassiopeia was a mythical queen who was turned into a constellation by a group of gods who favored her. She was then positioned in the sky by another group of gods who were her bitter rivals. These gods placed her so far north that she appeared upside-down for much of the year, a punishment for her vanity.

<u>Algae</u>

Also commonly seen on fringe forest mangrove snorkels are an abundance of algae with descriptive names such as Neptune's shaving brush, white scroll algae, mermaid's fan, and the sea pearl, an iridescent algae, which is one of the largest one-celled organism in the world. They can be as big as a ping pong ball.

Remember to respect the fragility of this most important environmental resource and enjoy!

blue tang

HAULOVER BAY

Haulover Bay offers seclusion, beautiful views, cool breezes and excellent snorkeling. The shoreline has varying characteristics. The western portion is rocky and has a small beach of coral and rock. On the eastern end of the bay, which can be reached by a ten-minute walk along the shoreline, you will find a narrow, coarse sand beach. Here the bottom is a mixture of sea grass, sand and coral rubble. The entire coast is lined with seagrape and maho trees interspersed between groups of large colorful rocks.

Arrival
Haulover Bay is 3.0 miles past the Coral Bay Moravian Church going east on the East End Road (Route 10). Park on the right side of the road alongside the small sand and coral rubble beach. See Map 6, page 274.

To reach the northern section of Haulover Bay, take the trail on the other (north) side of the road. It is an easy path about 100 yards long that goes over flat terrain.

The name
Haulover's name comes from its unique topographical characteristics. A narrow and flat strip of land separates Coral Bay on the south from Sir Francis Drake Channel on the north. It was, and still is, relatively easy to haul small boats over this stretch of land. The same journey by sea would involve sailing around the point at East End, which is notorious for strong currents, gusty winds and rough seas.

In the days of pirates and buccaneers a small vessel being pursued by a larger craft could "haul over" their boat to the other side, thus eluding the enemy whose vessel was too large to haul over and who would have to spend hours sailing around East End.

This feature of Haulover Bay was not only taken advantage of by pirates, but also by fishermen and others with boats small enough to make the overland journey practical.

Snorkeling - Northwestern side

This snorkel is best enjoyed on calm days and is recommended for strong swimmers, who have snorkeling experience. There is an element of danger due to the remoteness of the area as well as breaking waves and moderate currents. When the sea is rough, waves break along the shoreline, so be careful not to get pushed into the reef.

You can enter the water at the rock beach at the end of the trail. The water is shallow at first and the bottom is made up of small rocks and coral rubble. Watch out for black spiny sea urchins hiding here.

The reef rises up close to the surface near the shore and then slopes down to a depth of about thirty feet. There is an abundance of colorful hard coral such as star, brain, elkhorn, staghorn and pillar coral. Also plentiful are gorgonians, such as sea fan, sea plumes and dead man's fingers. Lobsters and eels can be found under ledges and in holes in the reef. Commonly seen fish on the reef are tang, snapper, grunts, parrotfish and angelfish.

Green turtles, stingrays and conch can be seen over the grassy areas, which make up most of the central portion of the bay.

Northeastern side

The eastern end of Haulover Bay can be reached by a ten-minute walk along the shoreline where you will find a small sand beach. When entering the shallow water, take care to avoid sea urchins and living coral.

Snorkel out along the eastern coast toward the point. Close to the shore are patches of sand and grass with scattered coral heads. The grass environment attracts rays, green turtles, starfish and conch.

There is a small fringe forest of mangroves along the coast. Just past these mangroves you will come to an underwater hillside garden of coral. This beautiful environment continues out and around the point. You will see many large, purple sea fans and other gorgonians as well as hard corals, such as star, elkhorn and brain coral. In some areas exquisite corals and sponges of every color imaginable encrust the underwater rock faces. Fish, such as parrotfish, snappers, jacks, grunts and schools of blue tang, abound just about everywhere along the reef as do anemones, feather duster worms, sea cucumbers and a myriad of other reef creatures. Look under ledges and in holes to see lobsters, eels and small fish seeking protection in their little hiding places.

Southern side
The snorkeling from Haulover Bay on St. John's southern shore is also enjoyable. This is the beach just off the road where you may have parked your vehicle. It is not as spectacular as the reef on the northern beach, but it is calmer, has an easier entry, and is more suitable for intermediate snorkelers.

Snorkel along the western shore toward the point and the off-shore rocks, called the blinders. Sea cucumbers are particularly plentiful here. Soft starfish, red urchins and bristle worms can be seen under the rocks in the shallow areas. Reef fish and an assortment of invertebrates can be found along the rocks and the fringing reef, which extends off the coast.

Right in the center of the bay, there is a patch reef that comes fairly close to the surface then drops down to a depth of about thirty feet. This area attracts many interesting fish and is a worthwhile place to explore.

BLUE COBBLESTONE BEACH
RAM HEAD TRAIL

The Blue Cobblestone Beach snorkel offers the opportunity to explore an underwater environment that usually occurs further offshore and in deeper waters. Here, protected by the hilly Ram Head Point, the seas are generally clear, calm and tranquil and the reef is colorful and diverse.

Arrival
From the Salt Pond Bay Parking lot, take the short trail down to the bay. Walk to the other end of beach and start out on the Ram Head Trail, which begins as a shoreline walk along the west side of the Ram Head Peninsula and take the trail as far as the Blue Cobblestone Beach. See Map 7, page 275.

Snorkeling
Enter the water at the north end of the beach near the large black rocks. The bottom is cobblestone and getting into the water is almost easy as from a sandy beach.

Begin by snorkeling around the large rocks at the corner of the beach. These rocks are encrusted with the mustard yellow fire coral, which can give snorkelers a mild sting if touched. There are also many colorful sponges and various types of hard coral in this area.

As you continue north around the point you will start to see underwater channels, known as spur and groove systems and the reef fringing the rocky coast gets larger, deeper and more colorful. At the seaward edge of this reef is a channel of sand about ten yards wide that separates the fringing reef from a neighboring patch reef farther offshore. The patch reef is surrounded by sand and lies in about twenty-five feet of water forming a pinnacle, which rises to a depth of about six feet.

This area is full of life, diverse and colorful. To fully appreciate it, the snorkeler should have the ability to pressurize and dive down in order to explore the lower areas of the reef.

There is a good deal of fire coral encrustation, but true hard coral varieties are also extremely plentiful. Look for pillar, star, staghorn, elkhorn and lettuce corals. Try to identify all the different colors of sponges found here. Gorgonians, such as sea fans, sea whips, sea rods and sea plumes grow on many sections of the reef and sway gracefully with the currents.

This healthy reef community is the habitat of many species of fish, including reef fish, grazing fish and fast swimming predators such as mackerel, yellowtail, blue runners and tarpon.

On the fringing reef across the sand channel from the patch reef is an area of coral outcropping called a ledge. Dive down and explore under the ledge to see different species of coral and interesting marine life.

The good snorkeling continues as you progress southward along the coast and towards the beach at Salt Pond Bay.

TEKTITE SNORKEL
BEEHIVE COVE

The Tektite snorkel is one of the absolute best snorkeling spots on the island of St. John, and, contrary to popular belief, it can be accessed by land with relative ease. The name, Tektite, refers to a research project conducted at Beehive Bay a small cove on the southeastern tip of Great Lameshur Bay

Arrival - Getting there is part of the fun

The first step is to get to Great Lameshur Bay on St. John's south coast. Take Salt Pond Road (Route 107) to the end of the pavement. Continue 0.6 mile on the dirt road. (A four-wheel drive vehicle is necessary on this steep and rutted track.) Park near the big tamarind tree at the entrance to this large secluded cobblestone beach. See Map 8, page 276.

Walk to the eastern end of the beach. A quarter-mile hike and rock scramble along the eastern shore of Cabritte Horn Point will take you to a remote and isolated coral rubble and sand beach called Donkey Bight. This bay, an inner bay of Great Lameshur, lies just to the north of Beehive Cove, the bay where the Tektite project took place.

There are no particularly difficult areas to negotiate. The hike, even carrying snorkel gear or light packs, is relatively easy, scenic, and just challenging enough to add a little excitement to the journey, without putting yourself in too much danger. Nevertheless, be careful and watch your footing at all times!

The beach at Donkey Bight can be a destination in itself. It is an idyllic little cove hardly ever frequented by anyone other than yachtsmen who may tie up to the single mooring located about thirty yards offshore.

Snorkeling

Put on your gear and enter the water from the sand on the southern end of the beach. Beehive Cove lies on the other side of the small rocky point to the south.

You will be snorkeling in a location that is somewhat far away from a convenient place to get out of the water, and there may be areas of rough seas. For these reasons this snorkel is recommended for experienced snorkelers only. For a full appreciation of this area, one should also have the ability to free dive in order to investigate the environments under ledges, beneath coral heads and within caves and tunnels. The snorkeling is best on calm days, when there is good visibility underwater.

Between Donkey Bight and Beehive Cove, you will find only scattered coral heads and small reefs, but there is usually an abundance of other interesting sea life such as tarpon, small reef fish, squid and sea cucumbers in this area.

As you approach Beehive Cove, the snorkeling becomes more exciting and more colorful. On the north side of the point there is a small cave with an exit to the surface. The walls and ceiling of the cave are covered with beautiful cup corals and sponges. As you snorkel around the point, or headland, which defines Beehive Bay, you will see a line of large rocks, which seems to attract a good share of fish.

On the Beehive Cove side of the point the water gets deeper. There are two rooms or chambers with rock walls on three sides. The second room is the most interesting, although both are beautiful. The eastern wall of the second room is encrusted with sponges and cup coral. Because there is low light within the room, some of the coral animals may have their tentacles extended as if it were night on the reef. The thin yellow tentacles protruding from the small bright orange cups make the corals look like flowers.

Further along there is a narrow channel in the rocks. On the eastern side is a cave with an outlet to the other side. There is at least one large dog snapper that likes to frequent this cave, and he is quite an impressive fellow. At the far end of the narrow channel is an exit to the other side over shallow coral. It is possible to snorkel over it, but great care must be taken, as there is usually a surge, which complicates things. Depending on the roughness of the sea, it may be better to explore the channel and then turn around and go back the way you came.

Around the next set of rocks is a wall encrusted with fire coral, sponges, and cup corals that descends to a depth of about twenty feet. Many small colorful fish can be seen along this wall, so take the time to look closely. On top of this rock, above the surface of the water, are concrete footings, which are all that remains of the Tektite project.

Further from shore you will see many beautiful coral heads, which are the basis of fascinating marine communities.

There is a wide diversity of fish in the general area, which include some of the fast swimming silvery fish such as mackerel, jack, tarpon and barracuda.

Although you may want to continue along the coast to explore the rocks around the next point called Cabritte Horn Point, remember that you are getting quite far from your starting point. A good time to return is after you pass the fire coral encrusted wall, where you can utilize the passage on the other side of the wall between the rocks and the shore as a loop for your U-turn.

The Tektite Project

The Tektite Project was conducted in 1969 in a cooperative effort by the U.S. Department of the interior, the U.S. Navy, The National Aeronautics and Space Administration (NASA), and General Electric. The purpose of the study was to investigate the effects on human beings of living and working underwater for prolonged periods of time.

The name of the project, Tektite, comes from a glassy meteorite that can be found on the sea bottom.

An underwater habitat, which was built by the General Electric Corporation and originally designed to be the model for the orbiting skylab, was placed on concrete footings fifty feet below the surface of Beehive Cove. It consisted of two eighteen-foot high towers joined together by a passageway.

Inside the towers were four circular rooms twelve feet in diameter. There was also a room, which served as a galley and a bunkhouse, a laboratory, and an engine room. The habitat was equipped with a hot shower, a fully equipped kitchen, blue window curtains, a radio and a television. A room on the lowest level called the wet room was where the divers could enter and leave the habitat through a hatch in the floor that always stayed open.

The four aquanauts, Ed Clifton, Conrad Mahnken, Richard Waller and John VanDerwalker, who took part in the first Tektite project lived under constant surveillance by cameras and microphones and often slept monitored by electroencephalogram (EEG) and electrocardiograms EKG to monitor their heart rates, brain waves and sleep patterns. The project lasted for 58 days and the men set a world record for time spent underwater, breaking the old record of thirty days held by astronaut Scott Carpenter in the Sea lab II habitat.

YAWZI POINT

This exciting and beautiful snorkel takes you around the rocky headland at Yawzi Point, the peninsula that separates Great and Little Lameshur Bays. The best snorkeling is relatively far from convenient entry and exit points. The seas can be choppy, and there can be some current. This snorkel should only be attempted by advanced snorkelers, and preferably, by those with the ability to free dive. It is also best to snorkel on calm days, or when the wind is out of the north.

Take the Yawzi Point Trail about half way to the end (0.2-mile). There will be a spur trail to the left that leads to a small well-hidden cove. Enter the water here and snorkel south towards the point. See Map 8, page 276.

All along this coast are a series of large rocks with beautiful coral encrustation. Further out, in deeper water, are patches of coral heads. There are many fish in the area and quite often you will see large tarpon, mackerels and barracuda.

At the rocky southern tip of the peninsula are steep large rocks, some of which extend above the surface. There are several classes of colorful hard corals, such as pillar, elkhorn, star and boulder coral. The rocks and coral heads are close together and form ledges, caves, arches, tunnels, grooves and channels. Corals and sponges encrust most of the rocky overhangs and undersides of tunnels and arches. One short tunnel has an extremely beautiful blue sponge encrustation on the rock walls at the entrance.

Sea fans, sea plumes and sea whips add to the spectacular underwater scenery.

Fish are extremely plentiful here. Watch for great schools of blue tang and other colorful reef fish.

You can return the way you came or continue around the point to the beach at Little Lameshur Bay. If you do continue on to Lameshur Bay, think about shoes for the walk back on the Yawzi Point Trail, notorious for small low-lying cactus, called suckers.

If there are beginners in your group, Little Lameshur has nice easy snorkeling around the rocks just off the beach in calm shallow water where they can snorkel while the more advanced snorkelers can explore Yawzi Point.

DITLEFF POINT SNORKEL

The sand and coral beach on the western side of Ditleff Point offers fine snorkeling for those of all levels of experience.

The water near shore is shallow and deepens gradually providing an easy entry over sand and seagrass.

For directions to the beach at Ditleff Point and for a description of the beach itself, see the chapter entitled "Ditleff Point Trail" and Map 10, page 278.

Beginners
Beginners can stay in the shallow grassy area just offshore or snorkel along the fringing reefs located on either side of the beach. Much of the coral is in good condition and colorful. There are many small fish to observe around and under the coral heads. The grassy area just off the beach is a habitat for turtles, squid, rays and starfish. If you see piles of shells around the coral reef, look for an octopus in nearby hole or crevice.

Intermediates
Those willing to venture out a little further can explore the undersea grasslands of Rendezvous Bay. There are acres of grasslands in the Ditleff Point and Rendezvous Bay area found in about fifteen feet of water. Although the basic environment does not change much, if you snorkel this area long enough, (about 10 - 15 minutes) you will begin to see the interesting animals that frequent the seagrass meadows. There are many green turtles here. The larger ones may be accompanied by remora who attach themselves to large sea creatures such as turtles or sharks. Also commonly seen here are rays. The southern stingray is dark gray in color, and it is often accompanied by a jack, who swims

just above the ray. There are also at least two large, impressive and graceful spotted eagle rays. They are black with white spots, have a defined head and a long thin tail. You may also find conch, starfish and squid. During the night, lobster and octopus come out of the reef and frequent the grasslands in search of food.

Advanced

One of the most exciting snorkeling areas on St. John can be found on the seaward side of the fringing reef, south of the beach. Beginning about half way between the beach and the southern tip of the point are a series of incredibly beautiful ledges formed by the outcropping of the coral. The base of the reef is in about 15 feet of water. The ceiling of the ledge ranges from about three to six feet and extends laterally approximately the same distance. To appreciate this area you must be able to dive down to the bottom and still have enough breath to explore under the ledge.

This is a unique and fascinating environment, combining the color and beauty of the various corals and sponges with an abundance of fish, eels, lobsters, octopus, shrimp, crabs, plume worms and other creatures which are attracted to the shelter of the ledge.

The rocky area at the end of the peninsula can be explored when the seas are calm and there is a minimum of surf breaking over the shallow reef. This extremely exciting area is only recommended for the experienced, confident and physically fit snorkeler.

Around and between the huge rocks are channels, arches, underwater canyons, chambers, tunnels and "painted" walls. As you will be in relatively open and unsheltered water, you will probably get to see bigger fish than those commonly found closer in.

PARROT BAY

The beach at Parrot Bay consists of soft white sand mixed with pieces of coral. There are scattered coral heads just offshore. There is often breaking surf and currents, so use caution if swimming or snorkeling here. Except for the westernmost extreme of the beach, there is a solid line of reef about twenty yards offshore that creates a shallow lagoon between the ocean and the beach.

Arrival
Take the South Shore Road (Route 104) to Fish Bay Road and continue to the intersection of Marina Drive and Reef Bay Road; bear left onto Reef Bay Road and go up the hill. Turn left after the concrete strip and proceed about a quarter mile further. Park across from the house with the wood shingle roof and sides. The path to the beach starts at the utility pole. See Map 9 page 277.

Privacy
Along the shoreline there are several patches of sand that jut into the vegetation providing a measure of privacy making Parrot Bay an ideal location for secluded sunbathing and picnicking.

Surfing
Surfers and boogie boarders can take advantage of the breaking southeasterly swells in the summer months, when there are no ground seas providing surfable waves on the north. The surfing and boogie boarding area is on the western end of the beach. Be careful of scattered coral heads, which sometimes are quite near the surface. Ask the locals for specific surfing information.

SEA TURTLES

Sea turtles are almost invariably a source of joy and excitement to the swimmers, snorkelers and divers fortunate enough to happen upon these gentle and magnificent creatures. Two species, the green turtle and the hawksbill turtle are commonly found around the Virgin Islands.

Green turtles are vegetarians and can usually be found grazing the seagrass beds in bays such as Maho, Francis, and Rendezvous.

Hawksbills have a distinctive hawk-like beak and are usually found around reefs where they hunt crabs, fish, and snails or use their sharp bill to scrape sponges, tube worms and encrusting organisms off rocks and coral.

The giant leatherback turtle also inhabits our waters, but is almost extinct and rarely seen. The leatherback can grow to as much as eight feet in length and weigh over 1000 pounds. Leatherbacks are so-named because, instead of having a hard shell like other sea turtles, their backs are protected by layers of leather-like plates. Leatherbacks live in deep water and subsist on a diet of jellyfish. A major threat to the leatherback comes in the form of improperly disposed plastic bags, which the leatherback may easily mistake for a jellyfish. If consumed, the plastic bag will kill the turtle by clogging up its intestines.

Sea turtles have been in existence for about 150 million years, inhabiting the tropical and subtropical seas of the world.

Even though these large reptiles spend almost all their life in the sea, they are air breathers. They hold their breath just like we do when we dive without tanks. Fortunately for the sea turtles, they can hold their breath much longer than we can. They are excellent swimmers, possessing large flippers that can propel their streamlined bodies through the water quickly and gracefully.

hawksbill turtle

Instead of teeth, sea turtles have a beak like a bird. (Like a hawk in the case of the hawksbill turtle.) Sea turtles have no ears, which is probably just as well for creatures that spend their whole life diving. They can still hear, however, accomplishing this through the use of eardrums that are conveniently covered with skin. Sea turtles have a keen sense of sight while they are under the water, but are quite nearsighted when they stick their heads out of the water for their breath of air. The turtles also have an excellent sense of smell, which also functions best while they are submerged.

The female sea turtle comes ashore on secluded beaches at night to lay her eggs. She then covers the eggs up with sand and does her best to cover up any traces of her nocturnal activities. The mother turtle returns to the sea while the eggs incubate, a process that takes about eight weeks. When the eggs hatch, the baby turtles dig their way out of the sand and crawl slowly towards the sea. They are very vulnerable at this time. The tiny turtles are easy prey. Moreover, they must avoid pitfalls such as getting trapped in holes in the sand, tangled up in seaweed, or having their way blocked by trash or other debris. They must reach the sea before the light of day exposes them to keen-eyed sea birds, mongooses, dogs, and the baking hot tropical sun.

No one knows for certain what the hatchlings do next, but many scientists believe that they then head out for the calm waters of the Sargasso Sea, which lies between the West Indies and the Azores in the middle of the Atlantic. Here they drift about hidden amidst the plentiful sargassum seaweed until they grow large enough to avoid most predators. The turtles then begin their long journey back to the beach where they were born. When the female reaches sexual maturity, sometime between 15 and 50 years depending on the species, she will lay her eggs on that beach.

The hawksbill, green and leatherback turtles are all listed as federally endangered species. Over-fishing and the commercial exploitation of hawksbills for tortoise shell products such as combs, hair barrettes, eyeglasses, picture frames and boxes have taken their toll on a once thriving population.

Sea turtles also face other serious problems. More and more beaches are being developed rendering them unsuitable for turtle nesting. Development also leads to an increase in the dog population. This is a problem because dogs are adept in finding and digging up turtle eggs. Furthermore it has been shown that mongooses do not instinctively hunt turtle eggs, but begin to do so after observing dogs engaged in this activity.

The awe and fascination that we experience upon an encounter with the sea turtle was shared by the cultures that inhabited these islands before us. To the spiritually evolved Taino people of the Caribbean, the turtle symbolized the ancestral mother and was a prominent feature in their religious art. This majestic and peaceful being cannot be allowed to become extinct. We must remember that we share our environment with all of God's creatures, and it is our responsibility to preserve and protect our unique heritage.

*This illustration courtesy of **Les Anderson***

CENTURY PLANT

Although many Virgin Islanders now purchase imported pine trees from North America to use as Christmas trees, the traditional Virgin Island Christmas tree is made from the stalk of the mature century plant.

The century plant is a common sight in St. John, especially in the drier areas of the island. It seems to stand up to all the challenges that these Virgin Islands can offer such as salt spray, steep hills, strong winds, poor soil, low rainfall and full sun.

Although the century plant resembles a giant aloe, it is in the Agave family, and more related to the cactus than to the aloe.

Christopher Columbus, on his first voyage to the West Indies, was fooled by the similarity. He had read the accounts of Marco Polo's journey to Asia, in which there was mention of the aloe, a valuable medicinal plant and worth a lot of money in Europe at that time. Consequently Columbus had his men gather a significant quantity of century plants and load them in the ships holds.

Cutting down, transporting and storing a large quantity of century plants was most likely an unpleasant task as the century plant is quite unfriendly to deal with. There are sharp hooked thorns all along the sides of the succulent leaves while the tips of the leaves end with long, straight and particularly sharp spines. The leaves are caustic and irritating to the skin when you (inevitably) get stuck with the spines.

After about ten or twenty years of life the century plant sends out a green stalk, which looks like a giant asparagus, from the center of the plant. The name century plant comes from a similar species found in the American desserts that blooms only once after one hundred years. The stalk grows rapidly, up to eight inches a day and can reach a height of over twenty feet. When the stalk reached its full height it produces branches with brilliant yellow flowers and pollen filled cups at the ends. This usually occurs around Easter. During the day the flowers attract hummingbirds, bananquits, moths, honeybees, bumblebees, dragonflies and wasps seeking the plentiful nectar of the blooms. At night the pollen filled cups and the unique aroma of the flowers attract bats that are excellent pollinators.

The stalk, branches and large seed brackets then turn brown, the leaves wither and the plant dies. The tall stalk, however, remains standing for quite a while.

Virgin Islanders have found several uses for the century plant stalk. For example, children sometimes tie the stalks together, employing whist vine or light rope, to make primitive rafts.

Also the sharp spine from the end of a mature succulent leaf can be extracted and if it is pulled out carefully it will emerge attached to a series of exceptionally strong fibers. The result is a needle and thread ready for use.

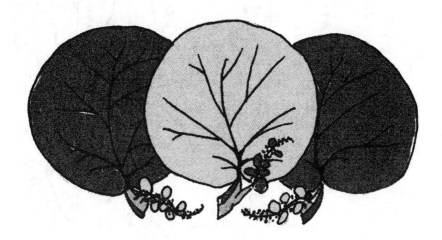

MAPS

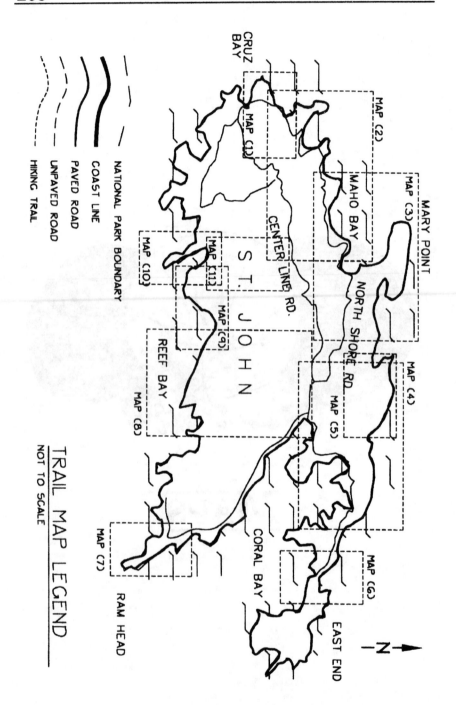

TRAIL MAP LEGEND
NOT TO SCALE

NATIONAL PARK BOUNDARY
COAST LINE
PAVED ROAD
UNPAVED ROAD
HIKING TRAIL

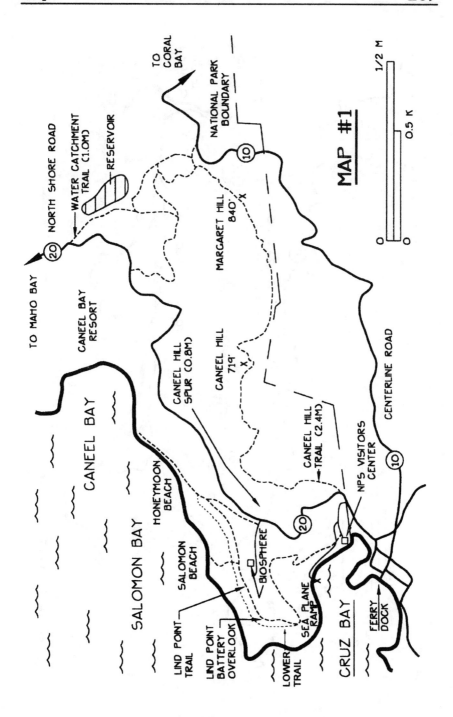

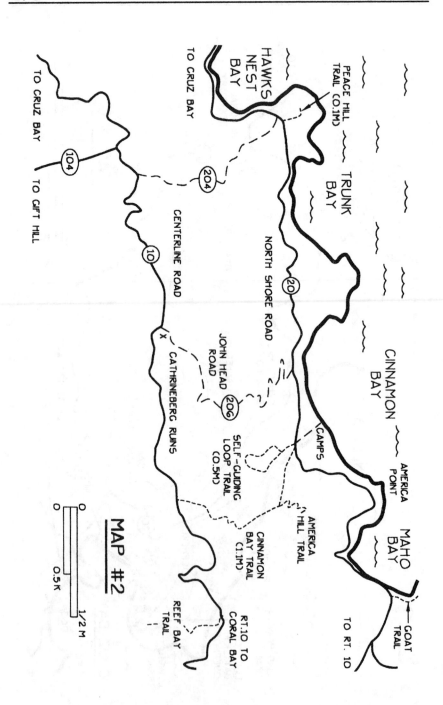

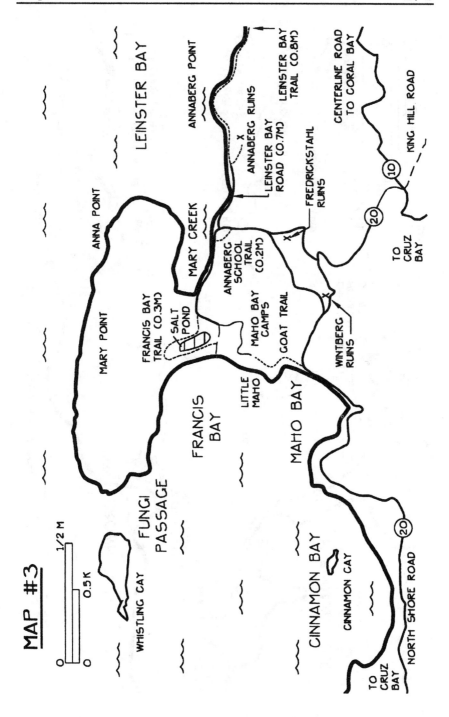

MAP #3

LEINSTER BAY

ANNABERG POINT

ANNABERG RUINS

LEINSTER BAY
TRAIL (0.8M)

LEINSTER BAY
ROAD (0.7M)

CENTERLINE ROAD
TO CORAL BAY

KING HILL ROAD

ANNA POINT

MARY CREEK

ANNABERG
SCHOOL
TRAIL
(0.2M)

FREDRICKSTAHL
RUINS

TO
CRUZ
BAY

MARY POINT

FRANCIS BAY
TRAIL (0.3M)

SALT
POND

MAHO BAY
CAMPS

GOAT TRAIL

WINTBERG
RUINS

LITTLE
MAHO

FRANCIS
BAY

MAHO BAY

FUNGI
PASSAGE

WHISTLING CAY

1/2 M

0.5 K

CINNAMON BAY

CINNAMON CAY

TO
CRUZ
BAY

NORTH SHORE ROAD

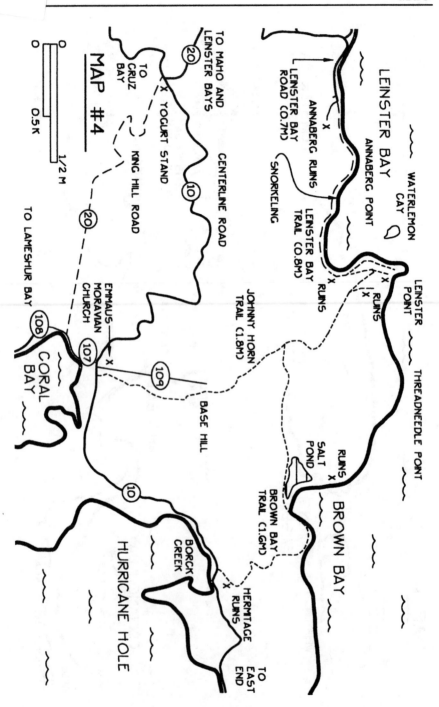

MAP #4

0   0.5 K
0   1/2 M

TO MAHO AND LEINSTER BAYS

TO CRUZ BAY

X YOGURT STAND

KING HILL ROAD

CENTERLINE ROAD

TO LAMESHUR BAY

EMMAUS MORAVIAN CHURCH X

CORAL BAY

BASE HILL

JOHNNY HORN TRAIL (1.8M)

LEINSTER BAY ROAD (0.7M)

ANNABERG RUINS X

SNORKELING

LEINSTER BAY TRAIL (0.8M)

RUINS X

RUINS X X

LEINSTER POINT

LEINSTER BAY

ANNABERG POINT

WATERLEMON CAY

THREADNEEDLE POINT

BROWN BAY

RUINS X

SALT POND

BROWN BAY TRAIL (1.6M)

TO EAST END

HERMITAGE RUINS X

BORCK CREEK

HURRICANE HOLE

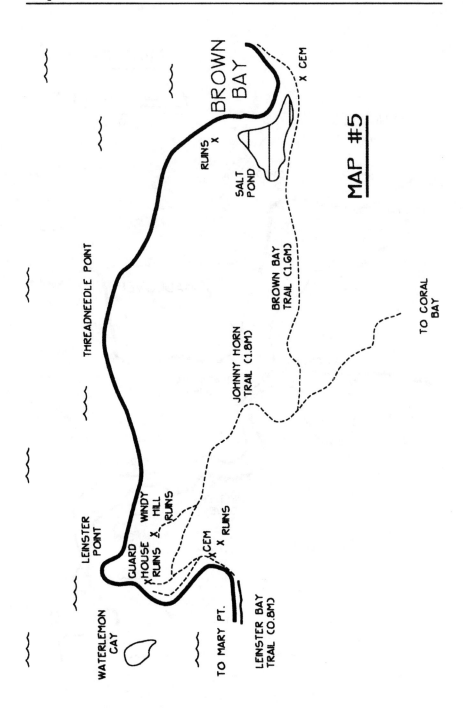

WATERLEMON CAY

LEINSTER POINT

THREADNEEDLE POINT

BROWN BAY

GUARD HOUSE RUINS X

WINDY HILL RUINS X

X CEM X RUNS

TO MARY PT.

LEINSTER BAY TRAIL (0.8M)

JOHNNY HORN TRAIL (1.8M)

RUINS X

SALT POND

X CEM

BROWN BAY TRAIL (1.6M)

TO CORAL BAY

MAP #5

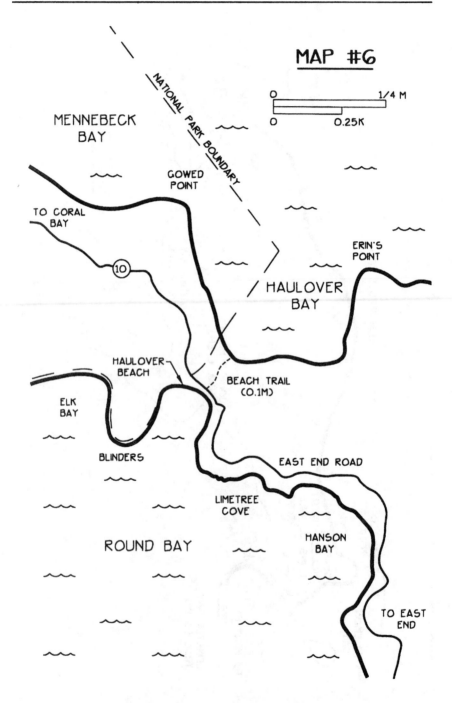

MAP #6

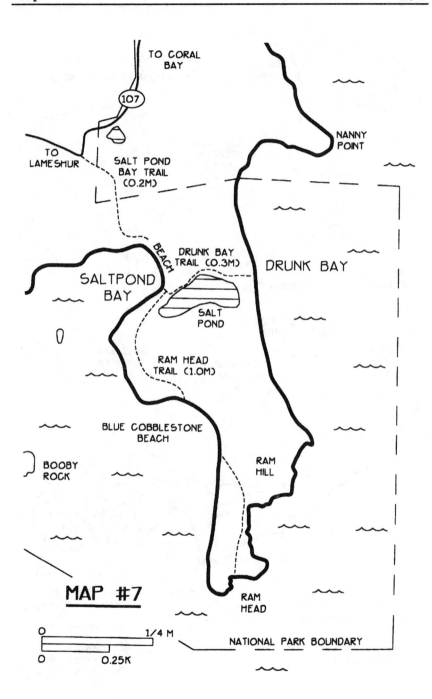

TO CORAL BAY

107

TO LAMESHUR

SALT POND BAY TRAIL (0.2M)

NANNY POINT

BEACH

DRUNK BAY TRAIL (0.3M)

DRUNK BAY

SALTPOND BAY

SALT POND

RAM HEAD TRAIL (1.0M)

BLUE COBBLESTONE BEACH

BOOBY ROCK

RAM HILL

MAP #7

RAM HEAD

0   1/4 M
0   0.25K

NATIONAL PARK BOUNDARY

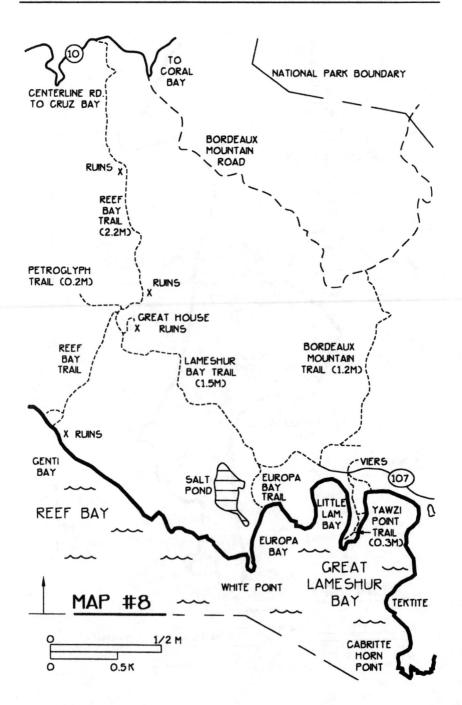

⑩

TO
CORAL
BAY

NATIONAL PARK BOUNDARY

CENTERLINE RD.
TO CRUZ BAY

BORDEAUX
MOUNTAIN
ROAD

RUINS X

REEF
BAY
TRAIL
(2.2M)

PETROGLYPH
TRAIL (0.2M)

RUINS
X

GREAT HOUSE
X   RUINS

REEF
BAY
TRAIL

LAMESHUR
BAY TRAIL
(1.5M)

BORDEAUX
MOUNTAIN
TRAIL (1.2M)

X RUINS

GENTI
BAY

VIERS

⑩⑦107

SALT
POND

EUROPA
BAY
TRAIL

LITTLE
LAM.
BAY

YAWZI
POINT
TRAIL
(0.3M)

REEF BAY

EUROPA
BAY

GREAT
LAMESHUR
BAY

MAP #8

WHITE POINT

TEKTITE

0   1/2 M

0   0.5 K

CABRITTE
HORN
POINT

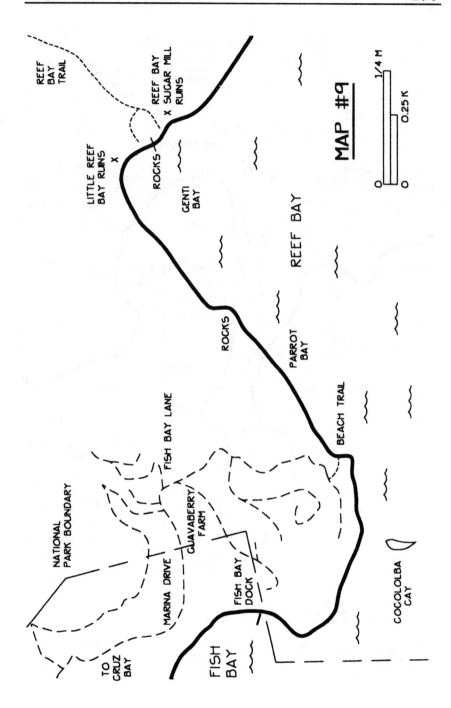

MAP #9

REEF BAY TRAIL

REEF BAY X SUGAR MILL RUINS

LITTLE REEF BAY RUINS X

ROCKS

GENTI BAY

REEF BAY

ROCKS

PARROT BAY

BEACH TRAIL

FISH BAY LANE

NATIONAL PARK BOUNDARY

GUAVABERRY FARM

MARINA DRIVE

TO CRUZ BAY

FISH BAY DOCK

FISH BAY

COCOLOLBA CAY

1/4 M

0.25 K

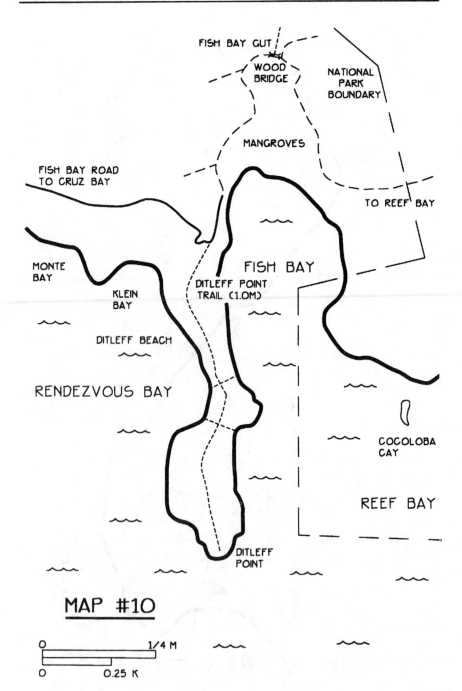

FISH BAY GUT

WOOD
BRIDGE

NATIONAL
PARK
BOUNDARY

MANGROVES

FISH BAY ROAD
TO CRUZ BAY

TO REEF BAY

MONTE
BAY

FISH BAY

KLEIN
BAY

DITLEFF POINT
TRAIL (1.0M)

DITLEFF BEACH

RENDEZVOUS BAY

COCOLOBA
CAY

REEF BAY

DITLEFF
POINT

MAP #10

O   1/4 M

O   0.25 K

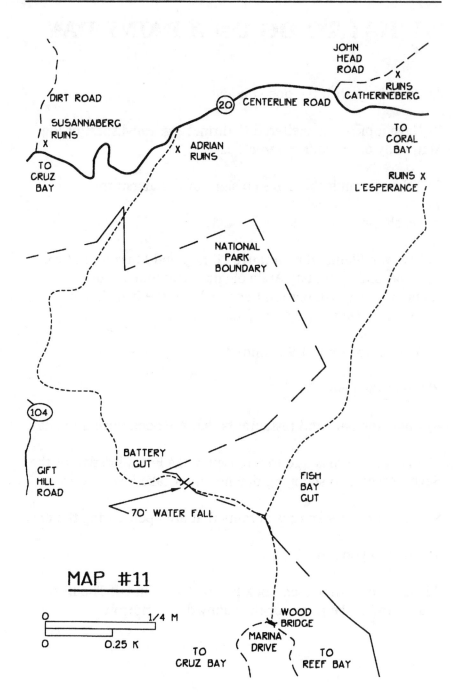

JOHN
HEAD
ROAD

DIRT ROAD

X
RUINS
CATHERINEBERG

⑳ CENTERLINE ROAD

SUSANNABERG
RUINS
X

TO
CORAL
BAY

X ADRIAN
RUINS

TO
CRUZ
BAY

RUINS X
L'ESPERANCE

NATIONAL
PARK
BOUNDARY

⑩④

GIFT
HILL
ROAD

BATTERY
GUT

FISH
BAY
GUT

70' WATER FALL

MAP #11

0
1/4 M

0
0.25 K

WOOD
BRIDGE

MARINA
DRIVE

TO
CRUZ BAY

TO
REEF BAY

WHAT TO DO ON A RAINY DAY

1) Cuddle up with the one you love.

2) Have a picnic at sheltered Cathrineberg, Hawksnest or Big Maho Bay or on your covered deck.

3) Take a swim if there are no signs of thunderstorms.

4) Go shopping.

5) Visit the Elaine Ione Sprauve Library and Museum in Cruz Bay, the Cinnamon Bay Archeological Museum at the Cinnamon Bay Campground or check out the Ivan Jadan Museum on Genip Street in Cruz Bay.

6) Take a taxi tour of St. John.

7) Go to the gym.

8) Enjoy the bars and restaurants that are open during the day.

9) Visit St. Thomas - go to a museum like Fort Christian or the Seven Arches, go shopping downtown or take a land tour.

9) Go to the bars and restaurants that are open during the day.

10) Rent a good movie.

11) Curl up with a good book like or "St. John Off The Beaten Track" and make plans for the sunny day tomorrow.

CHRONOLOGY

100,000,000 - BC Rocky core of St. John first laid down on the ocean floor as a result of subterranean volcanic activity produces rocks found at Ram Head.

15,000 BC - Glaciers lower the sea level over 300 feet and St. John is connected to Puerto Rico and the rest of the northern Virgin Islands. What is now ocean shelf was grasslands, savannas and scrub forests.

5000 BC - Melting of the glaciers results in the separation of the islands.

1000 BC - First people migrate to St. John. Pre-ceramic culture settled on south shore (from South America)

20 AD - Second wave of migrants arrive in St. John (pre-Taino culture from South America).

1000 - 1492 - Taino culture dominates St. John (from Hispaniola).

1493 - Columbus sails by St. John; no inhabitants reported.

1511 - 1530 - St. John re-occupied by Tainos escaping from persecution in Puerto Rico and St. Croix.

1555 - Remaining Tainos driven away from the Virgin Islands after Charles V of Spain ordered that they be treated as enemies and exterminated.

1671 - 1717 - St. John inhabited from time to time by small groups of woodcutters, sailors and farmers.

1672 - Danes settle St. Thomas.

1684 - English thwart Danish attempts to settle St. John.

1718 - First permanent settlement at Coral Bay by Danish West India Company.

1718 - 1850 - Plantation Era

1728 - 87 plantations: 123 whites, 677 blacks

1733 - St. John is the victim of a severe drought, insect plague and a devastating hurricane.
Merciless slave code imposed (September 5).

109 plantations: 208 whites, 1,087 blacks.

Slave insurrection at Fortsberg (November 23).

1734 - French troops from Martinique quell rebellion.

1739 - Plantation system on St. John returns to the pre-rebellion levels;109 plantations: 208 whites, 1414 blacks.

1755 - King Frederick of Denmark buys all the land, slaves, estates, ships, factories and everything else that was owned by the Danish West India Company and brings company rule of St. John and the rest of the Danish West Indies to an end.

Frederik V issues the Reglement of 1755 in which slave rights were mentioned for the first time. (Not published on St. John).

1766 - St. John and St. Thomas were declared free ports by the Danish Crown.

Plans were made to take advantage of the excellent harbor at Coral Bay and to begin the development of a town there. Land in the Coral Bay area was even divided up into town lots. This hoped for development did not materialize, and St. John remained primarily rural until the recent growth of tourism.

1773 - The population on St. John includes 2330 slaves and 104 whites. There are 69 plantations, 42 of which are devoted to cotton. (From report ordered by governor Kragh of the Danish West Indies)

1782 - H.M.S. Santa Monica holed; beached at Round Bay, East End.

1783 - Moravians establish second mission at Emmaus.

1792 - Slave trade law passed, African slave trade to end in ten years.

1801 - Three month British occupation.

1802 - Denmark abolishes the slave trade.

1807-15 - British reoccupation.

1808 Law outlawing slave trade goes into effect in the Danish West Indies. (Denmark becomes the first European nation to abolish the slave trade; 123,000 slaves had been brought from Africa to the D.W.I. by that time).

1834 - Emancipation of British Virgin Islands offers St. John slaves an escape opportunity.

1840 - Major escape to the British Virgin Islands by slaves from Leinster Bay and Annaberg, followed a few days later by slaves from Adrian, Brown Bay and Hermitage

1841 - St. John population high point 2,555 (pre-modern).

1844 - Mary Point School completed.

1846 - Population: 2450, 1790 slaves, 660 free (including whites).

1848 - July 3; Emancipation of slaves in the Danish West Indies
July 4; News reaches St. John.
July 5; Police placard posted in Cruz Bay prohibiting the "freed" from leaving the island.
July 10; Police placard posted in Cruz Bay compelling the "freed" to sign labor contracts with their former owners.

1848 - 1950 - Peasant Era

1849 - Labor Act forces freed slaves to stay on plantations.

1854 - Cholera epidemic kills 218

1855 - Population 1715

1856 - Two cholera epidemics ravage population.

1859 - Moravians stop baptizing children born out of wedlock.

1862 - East End School constructed.

1867 - Devastating hurricane followed by earthquake severely damages estates and crops, serves to end the plantation system

1868 - 205 voters unanimous in favor of United States purchase.

1868 - United States rejects purchase of St. Thomas and St. John from Denmark for $7.5 million

1878 - Carolina Plantation in Coral Bay acquired by William Henry Marsh

1878 - Mary Thomas (Queen Mary) leads rebellion of disgruntled workers.

1879 - Labor Act amended to allow contract negotiation.

1880 - Widow George rented room by the night at in her house at Newfound Bay.
Population 994

1900 - Population 925

1902 - Denmark rejects United States offer to buy St. Thomas, St. John and St. Croix for $5 million.

1907 - J.P. Jorgenson wrote the Short Guide to St. Thomas and St. Jan, a travel guide written in English

1917 - Official transfer of Danish West Indies to United States; March 31, for $25,000,000.

1917 - Virgin Islands put in charge of U.S. Navy.

1918-19 - Reef Bay factory closing ends sugar production.

1921 - United States Virgin Island flag adopted.

1927 - Virgin Islanders granted American citizenship

1929 - Erva and Paul Boulon Sr. buy Trunk Bay and 100 additional acres of land for $2500.

1930 - First automobile (Lito Vals).

1930 - St. Thomas Daily News founded.

1930 - Average wage in Virgin Islands is 40 cents a day.

1930 - Navy rule ended.

1931 - First civilian governor, Dr. Paul M. Pearson.

1936 - Organic Act passed.

1936 - Danish West India Company opens Caneel Bay resort.

1939 - St. John mentioned by Harold Huber of National Park Service in N.P.S. report as possible park. The onset of World War II causes the plan to be shelved.

1946 - First black governor William H. Hastie

1946 - Robert and Nancy Gibney come to St. John on Honeymoon.

1948 - First jeep brought to the island on a sloop from St. Thomas (Ron Morrisette Sr.).

1950 - St. John population declines to 746.

1950 - Present - Tourism Era

1950 - Robert and Nancy Gibney buy property at Hawksnest.

1953 - 14 Jeeps registered on St. John; Island administrator proposes "limiting the number and size of vehicles on the island (annual report of the administrator 1953).

1956 - 53 Jeeps, 31trucks, 5 station wagons (annual report of the administrator 1956).

1954 - Laurance Rockefeller begins acquiring land on St. John.

1954 - Organic Act passed giving some measure of independence to the Virgin Islands

1955 - Only 56 acres out of 12,160 acres in cultivation; 85% is second growth forest.
Rockefeller addresses the Senate Subcommittee on Territories and Insular Affairs. Rockefeller says that St. John had "had the most superb beaches and view" and was "the most beautiful island in the Caribbean."

1956 - Virgin Islands National Park opens; 5,000-acre gift of Jackson Hole Preserve.
Caneel Bay Plantation reopens.
Twenty-four-hour electrical service inaugurated

1957 - Gibneys sell a parcel of beachfront land to J. Robert Oppenheimer, "the Father of the Atomic Bomb."

1959 - Virgin Islands National Park acquires Trunk Bay from the Boulon family

1962 - 5560 acres of submerged lands are transferred to the jurisdiction of the National Park.
First commercial jet lands in St. Thomas (Pan Am).

1966 Pan Am begins direct flights to U.S. mainland.

1967 Antilles airboats begin seaplane service with flights to St. John

1969 - Project Tektite in Great Lameshur Bay (Underwater Habitat)

1971 - Melvin Evans first black Virgin Islander to be elected governor

1971 Virgin Islands are the first U.S. state or territory to observe Rev. Dr. Martin Luther King's birthday as a legal holiday.

1978 - Mongoose Junction Opens

1989 - Hurricane Hugo (September)

1994 - 1,200,000 visitors to St. John National Park

1995 - Hurricane Marilyn (September) 10 killed in Virgin Islands
      $1.5 billion in damages.
      Seaplane service to St. John discontinued due to
      damages sustained and subsequent announcement by the
      National Park Service saying they will no longer allow
      use of seaplane ramp

1997 - Dr. Donna Christian Green first woman to be elected
      Virgin Islands delegate to U.S. Congress.

BIBLIOGRAPHY

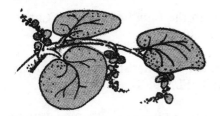

St. John People, American Paradise Publishing, St. John,U.S.V.I., 1993

*Taino,*The Montacelli Press, El Museo del Barrio 1997

Anderson, John Lorenzo; *Night of the Silent Drums,* Mapes Monde Editore, St. Thomas, U.S.V.I., 1992

Barlow, Virginia; *The Nature of the Islands,* Chris Doyle Publishing and Cruising Guide Publications, Dunedin, FL, 1993

De Booy and Faris; *Our New Possessions,* J.B. Lippincott Co., Philadelphia, PA and London, 1918

Dookhan, Issac *A History of the Virgin Islands of the United States,* Canoe Press, 1994

Hall,Neville A. T.; *Slave Society in the Danish West Indies,* University of the West Indies Press, Jamaica, W.I. 1992

Guirty, Geraldo; *Sixtonian,* Vantage Press, NY, 1991

Hatch, Charles; *St. John Island ("The Quiet Place"),* Virgin Islands National Park, Denver, CO, 1972

Jadan, Doris; *A Guide to The Natural History of St. John,* Environmental Studies Inc., U.S.V.I., 1985

Koladis, Randall S.; *St. John on Foot and by Car,* 1974

Low, Ruth Hull and Vals; Rafael; *St. John Backtime*, Eden Hill Press, St. John U.S.V.I., 1985

Morrisette, Ronald A.; *A Little Guide to the Island of St. John*, Caneel Bay Plantation, St. John, U.S.V.I., 12/16/67

Olwig, Karen Fog; *Cultural Adaptation and Resistance on St. John*, University of Florida Press, Gainesville, FL, 1985

Paiewinsky, Isador; *Eyewitness Accounts of Slavery in the Danish West Indies*, Fordham University Press, NY, 1989

Robinson, Alan H.; *Virgin Islands National Park*, KC Publications, Las Vegas, Nevada, 1974

Rouse, Irving; *The Tainos.* Yale University Press, 1992

Stark, Charlotte Dean; *Some True Tales and Legends About Caneel Bay, Trunk Bay And a Hundred and One Other Places on St. John*, St. John, U.S.V.I., 1960

Trollope, Anthony; *The West Indies and the Spanish Main*, Hippocrene Books, 1985

Tyson George F. and Highfield, Arnold R.; *The Danish West Indian Slave Trade*, Virgin Islands Humanities Council, U.S.V.I., 1994

Tyson George F. and Highfield, Arnold R.; *The Kamina Folk*, Virgin Islands Humanities Council, U.S.V.I., 1994

Zabriskie, Luther K.; *The United States Virgin Islands*, G. P. Putnam and Sons, New York, 1918

Recommended Reading:
Feet Fins and Four Wheel Drive, by Pam Gaffin